SABAD and
PUNJABI
Songs' Western Notes
Part-1

Notations writer: Vinod Kumar

Notion Press

NOTION PRESS

India. Singapore. Malaysia.

ISBN xxx-x-xxxxx-xx-x

Vinod Kumar

DEDICATION

This book is dedicated to my Parents.

-Vinod Kumar

CONTENTS

PRAYERS

Guru Nanak Dev Ji

This life is four day's fair. Do not waste it. You have got this human body fortunately. Make this life better by God worship. Life is running. Have sometime to pray Ishwar. At last nothing will go with you. Your prayers and good work will accompany you and take you accros this world's ocean. Sing Sabad for the purpose.

 Also Punjabi Songs are very melodious and make everybody happy and joyful. Who sings, gets its taste.

Waheguru ji

-Vinod Kumar

PREFACE

My hearty greetings and Namaste to Readers. I have written 51 Songs' Sargam books of Mukesh-1,2, Kishor-1,2, Lata, Asha, Manna dey, Yesudas, Kumar Shanu, Rafi-1,2,3,4 and SD Burman's composed song book in Hindi Language and translated many books in English SARGAM and Western CDEFG. Bhajan Swarlipi 1,2,3 and one Gazal Sargam book is also published in Hindi, English and Western notes. All these books are available online. Now I have written and translated the book as Sabad and Punjabi Songs' Western Notes, Part-1 book. Lyrics are in English and notations in CDEF style, so that music lovers can play and sing songs and get enjoyed.

Mostly song's notations are written in original scale but somewhere you have to transpose +1 or − 1 or +2 to get original scale. Sa taken is also mentioned in each song's detail. Person who knows western notations can understand as given below:

.नी	.नी	सा	रे	रे	ग	ग	म
.$\underline{N}$	.N	S	$\underline{R}$	R	$\underline{G}$	G	M
.B^b	.B	C	D^b	D	E^b	E	F
.$A^{\#}$	.B	C	$C^{\#}$	D	$D^{\#}$	E	F

मे	प	ध	ध	नी	नी	सां	रें
M*	P	$\underline{D}$	D	$\underline{N}$	N	S'	R'
G^b	G	A^b	A	B^b	B	C'	$D^{b'}$
$F^{\#}$	G	$G^{\#}$	A	$A^{\#}$	B	C'	$C^{\#'}$

In this book some symbols are given as (G-) it means you have to play G for two beats duration or matra similarly you have to play for the beats for more number of – if there are more dashes. When two notes are written adjacending to each other it means you have to play the notes in one beat or matra as MP mapa is played in one beat.

Notations at the beginning of the song are prelude and notations in the middle of the song are interlude. These notations are written by me by my experience. Hope readers shall understand, like and enjoy it. A person having basic knowledge of music can play the songs on any instrument.

One has to practice sargam daily and its palte also so that one can become expert in playing difficult notes sequence. People can enjoy your playing instruments and then only your success will be counted. Care has been taken to provide accuracy still there is no liability of correctness and accuracy of notes and writer, printer, publisher and editor is not respoinsible for any error or ommissions or mistakes. If any mistake is found kindly inform.

For purchasing the books in India, one can visit notionpress.com or flipkart.com and amazon.in. Kindly review my books at amazon and flipkart and give proper stars after purchasing my books from the above sites. For any query, email to me.

- Vinod Kumar (vinod66vk@gmail.com)

SARGAM

SARGAM swars/sound are derived from voice of animals and birds. C scale is as follows:-

Note Name	Swar	स्वर नाम	Swar full name	स्वर का पूरा नाम हिंदी में	यह स्वर किस पशु पक्षी की आवाज से लिया गया है.
C=	Sa=	सा	Shadaj	षडज	Peacock/ मोर की आवाज़
D=	Re=	रे	Rishabh	रिषभ	Papiha /पपीहा की आवाज़
E=	Ga=	ग	Gandhar	गन्धार	Goat/ बकरा की आवाज़
F=	Ma=	म	Madhyam	मध्यम	Crane/ बगुला की आवाज़
G=	Pa=	प	Pancham	पंचम	Koccoo/Koyal/ कोयल की आवाज़
A=	Dha=	ध	Dhaiwat	धैवत	Frog/ दादुर या मेंढक की आवाज़
B=	Ni=	नी	Nishad	निषाद	Elephant हाथी की आवाज़
C'=	Sa'=	सां	(Higher Sa)		

C#=$\underline{Re}$=रे॒ (रे कोमल), D#=$\underline{Ga}$=ग॒ (ग कोमल), F#=Ma*=मे (म तीव्र), G#=$\underline{Dha}$=D (D कोमल), A#=$\underline{Ni}$=नी॒ (नी कोमल)

We can write as S $\underline{R}$ R $\underline{G}$ G M M* P $\underline{D}$ D $\underline{N}$ N S'

All notes underlined are called Komal Swar as Komal Re Komal Ga Komal Dha Komal Ni. One note Ma* is called Tivra Ma Sequence of the notes are-

S	$\underline{R}$	R	$\underline{G}$	G	M	M*
सा	रे॒	रे	ग॒	ग	म	मे
C	D^b	D	E^b	E	F	G^b
C	$C^\#$	D	$D^\#$	E	F	$F^\#$

P	$\underline{D}$	D	$\underline{N}$	N	S'
प	ध॒	ध	नी॒	नी	सां
G	A^b	A	B^b	B	C'
G	$G^\#$	A	$A^\#$	B	C'

Vinod Kumar

Sa and Pa are Achal Swar (fixed notes). They do not have any Komal or Tivra. They are fixed notes as per North Indian music tradition.

OCTAVE

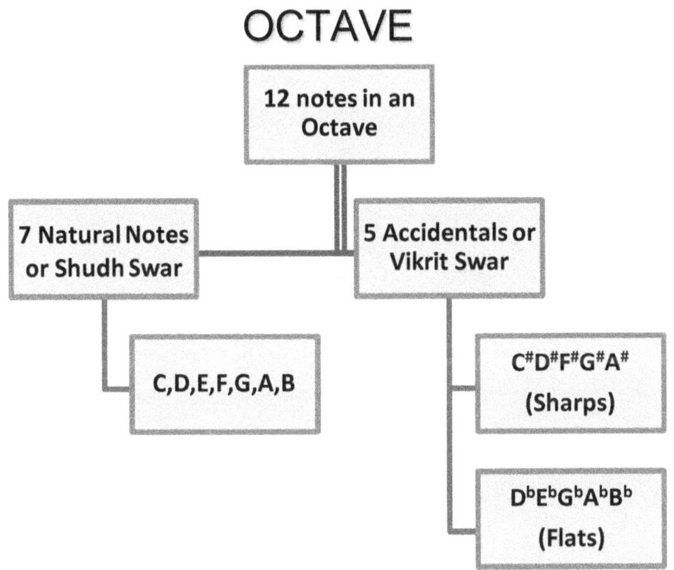

Sequence of the notes on any instrument are:

.B♭ .B C D♭ D E♭ E F G♭ G A♭ A B♭ B C′ D♭′ D′ so on…

.A# .B C C# D D# E F F# G G# A A# B C′ C#′ D′ D#′

C Scale is given as: **C D E F G A B C′**

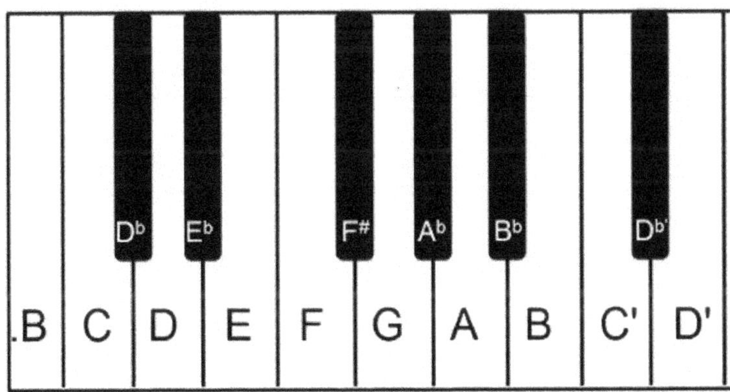

Sabad and Punjabi Songs' Western Notes, Part-1

$C^{\#}$ Scale is given as:

$C^{\#}$ $D^{\#}$ F $F^{\#}$ $G^{\#}$ $A^{\#}$ C′ $C^{\#\prime}$

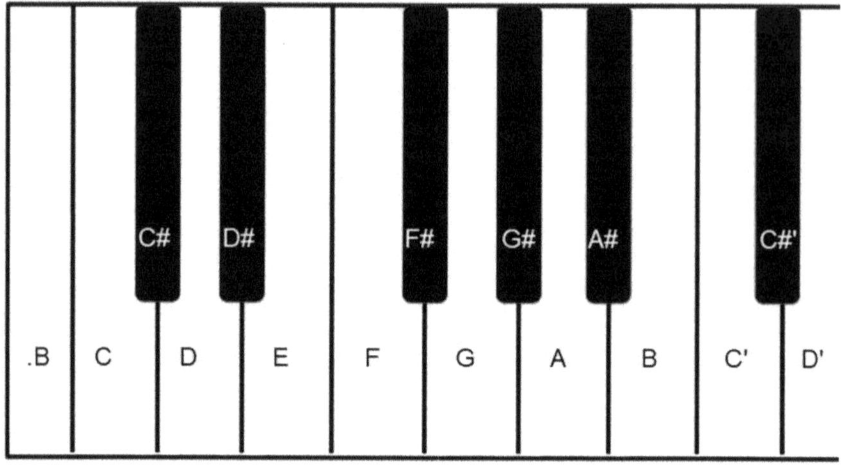

Vinod Kumar

1.   BAHEIN JINNA DI PAKADIYE

Sabad

Film: Silsila (1981)

Taal: Kaharwa

Music: Shiv Kumar Sharma,

Hari Prasad Chaurasia (Shiv-Hari)

Singer: Raagi

Chord: EGB   S=C

https://www.youtube.com/watch?v=oWEelVb35YA

bahein jinna di pakadiye, sir deejai baahein na chhodiye

chit charan kamal ka aasra, chit charan kamal sang jodiye

man loche pur aaiyaan, gur shab deekhe man hodiye

teg bahadur boleya, dhar piye dharam na chhodiye

BAHEIN JINNA DI PAKADIYE

dha	ge	n	ti	n	ke	dhi	n	dha	ge	n	ti	n	ke	dhi	n
1	2	3	4	5	6	7	8	1	2	3	4	5	6	7	8

prelude:
flute: BG AF$^\#$ GE F$^\#$G A-
sarangi: F$^\#$GG-E EF$^\#$F$^\#$-DE-
            F$^\#$ F$^\#$GG-E EF$^\#$F$^\#$-D E-
            E G A B--

BA   GA   F$^\#$ DDEE   BD^{b}' D' D^{b}'B D^{b}'B A   ABB
bahein jinna di pakadiye, sir   deejai baahein na chhodiye

BD^{b}'   D' D^{b}'B   D^{b}'B   A   ABB –GAF$^\#$
sir   deejai baahein na chhodiye

BD^{b}' D'E'E' E'D'D' BD^{b}' D'E'E' BD^{b}' D'D'D^{b}' BD^{b}'D^{b}' BA ABB
chit charan kamal ka   aasra, chit charan kamal sang jodiye

BA   GA   F$^\#$ DDEE
bahein jinna di   pakadiye

D'E' E'D' BD^{b}' D'E'E'   D^{b}'D^{b}' D'D' D^{b}'BD^{b}' BA ABB-GAF$^\#$
man loche pur aaiyaan, gur   shab deekhe man hodiye

BA   GA   F$^\#$ DDEE
bahein jinna di   pakadiye

E'E' E'D'BD'   D'E'E' D'   D'D'D^{b}'B D^{b}'D^{b}'B A   ABB
 teg   bahadur boleya, dhar piye   dharam   na chhodiye

BD^{b}' D'D'D'D^{b}'B   D^{b}'D^{b}'B A ABB- GAF$^\#$
dhar piye   dharam na chhodiye

BA   GA   F$^\#$ DDEE
bahein jinna di   pakadiye

Vinod Kumar

2. BEGAMPURA SAHAR KO NAU

Sabad: Bhagat Ravi Das Ji
Taal: Kaharwa
Transpose+1 and play from C Scale
https://youtu.be/p9GSOWCDmkA

Singer: Bhai Sarbjit Singh ji
Chord: DFA   S=C#

begampura sahar ko nau

dukhu andoh nahi tihi thau

naan tasvees khiraju na malu

khauf na khata na tarasu jawalu

ab mohi khub vatan gah paayi

uhaan khairi sadaa mere bhai

kaimu daaimu sadaa paatisahi

dom na sem ek so aahi

aabaadaanu sadaa mashoor

uhaan gani basahi maamur

tiu tiu sail karahi jiu bhave

mahram mahal n ko atkave

kahi ravidas khalaas chamaaraa

jo ham sahrii su meetu hamaaraa

BEGAMPURA SAHAR KO NAU

dha	ge	n	ti	n	ke	dhi	n	dha	ge	n	ti	n	ke	dhi	n
1	2	3	4	5	6	7	8	1	2	3	4	5	6	7	8

prelude:
 C.AD CD DDE FE DCD
begampura sahar ko nau

AG   FA-G GG FE G-F
dukhu andoh nahi tihi   thau

$B^b B^b$ $B^b B^b$G FE DC   DD
dukhu andoh nahi tihi   thau

B   BABB BBB   A BG
naan tasvees khiraju na malu

C'C' C' C'D'B A GFG   G A
khauf na khata na tarasu jawalu

E'   E'D'E'E'   C'AC' C' D'D'
naan tasvees   khiraju na malu

D'C'   B AGF F FGF E DD
khauf na khata na tarasu jawalu

BB BA BB BBB BA BG
ab mohi khub vatan gah paayi

C'C' C'C'D' GF GG   AA
uhaan khairi sadaa mere bhai

E'E' E'D' E'E' C'AA C'C' D'D'
ab   mohi   khub vatan gah paayi

C'A   FGE GG^A FE   DD
uhaan khairi sadaa mere bhai

BBA B-GG BB   BABG
kaimu daaimu sadaa paatisahi

Vinod Kumar

C'C' C' C'-D' FF G AA
dom na sem ek so aahi

E'D' E'E' C'A C'C'D'D'
aabaadaanu sadaa mashoor

C'A FGE FG EDD
uhaan gani basahi maamur

B BA BG BBB BA B-G
tiu tiu sail karahi jiu bhave

C' C' C'C'D'D' A F GG AA
mahram mahal n ko atkave

E'E' E'D'E'E' C'AC' C'D'D'
kahi ravidas khalaas chamaaraa

C' AG FGE F GF EDD
jo ham sahrii su meetu hamaaraa

3.   DUKH BHANJAN TERA NAAM JI

Sabad   Taal: Kaharwa   Singer: Bhai Ravinder Singh ji
Transpose+3 and play from C Scale   Chord: .BDG   S=D#
https://youtu.be/2zXn2NqWWYI

dukh bhanjan tera naam ji, dukh bhanjan tera naam
aath pahar aaraadhiye puran satgur gyan

jit ghat vase paarbrahm soi suhava thau
jam knkar ned n aavai o rasna hari gun gau

seva surat n jaaniyaan n jaape aaraadh
ot teri jag jeevnaa mere thakur agam agaadh

bhaye kirpaal gosaaiyaan natthe sok santaap
tatti wau n lagai satgur rakkhe aap

gur narayan day gur gur sachcha sirjan haar
gur tutthe sabh kuch paaiya jan naanak sad balhaar

DUKH BHANJAN TERA NAAM JI

dha	ge	n	ti	n	ke	dhi	n	dha	ge	n	ti	n	ke	dhi	n
1	2	3	4	5	6	7	8	1	2	3	4	5	6	7	8

C.B CDD G-F$^{\#}$ E-D ED   C.B CDD   F$^{\#}$-E   D--
dukh bhanjan tera   naam ji,   dukh bhanjan tera   naam

 B   BB   AABAG   C'B AGAF$^{\#}$ G- EF$^{\#}$ED
aath pahar aaraadhiye puran satgur   gyan

BB BB BC'B C'D'D'D'   D'D' C'BAC'B B---AG
jit ghat vase paarbrahm   soi   suhava   thau

 B   BBB BC' B C'D'D' C'D'C' BA   C'B B---AG
jam knkar ned n aavai   rasna hari gun gau

Vinod Kumar

B   BB   AABAG   C'B   AGAF$^{\#}$ G- EF$^{\#}$ED
aath pahar aaraadhiye puran satgur   gyan

C.B   CDD   G-F$^{\#}$ E-D   ED   C.B   CDD   F$^{\#}$-E   D--
dukh bhanjan tera   naam ji,   dukh bhanjan tera   naam

BB   BB   BC'B C'D'D'D' D'D' C'BAC'B B---AG
bhaye kirpaal gosaaiyaan   natthe sok   santaap

 BB BBC' B C'D'D'   D'   C'BA C'BB---AG
 seva surat n jaaniyaan n   jaape aaraadh

 B BB C'B C'D'D'   D'   D'D'C'   BAC'   BBB---AG
 ot   teri jag jeevnaa mere thakur agam   agaadh

B   B B   C'BC'D'D'   D'C'   BAC'   BBB---AG
bhaye kirpaal gosaaiyaan natthe sok   santaap

BB BC' B C'D'D'   C'D'C'B A C'B BB---AG
 tatti wau n lagai   satgur   rakkhe aap

B BB-C'B C'   D'D'   D'   D'C'   BAC'B BB---AG
gur narayan day gur   gur sachcha sirjan   haar

 B BB   BB C'B C'D'D' D' D'C'C' BA C'BBB---AG
 gur tutthe sabh kuch paaiya jan naanak sad   balhaar

4.   EK ONKAR SATNAM

Singer: Ms Pooja   Chord: CEG   S=D

Transpose+2 and play from C Scale

https://youtu.be/LbftHnxqUfk

ek onkar, sat naam

karta purakh

nirbhau nirbair

akaal murat

ajuni saibham

gur parsad

japu aadi sach jugadi sach

hai bhi sach, naanak hosi bhi sach

sochai sochi n hovaii, je soche lakh vaar

chuppai chup n hovaii, je laai raha livtaar

bhukhiya bhukh n utari, je banna puriya bhar

sahas siyanpa lakh hohi, ta ik na challe naali

kiv sachiyara hoiai, kiv kude tutte paali

hukum rajai chalna, naanak likhiya naali

Vinod Kumar

EK ONKAR SATNAM

dha	ge	n	ti	n	ke	dhi	n	dha	ge	n	ti	n	ke	dhi	n
1	2	3	4	5	6	7	8	1	2	3	4	5	6	7	8

CD   CCC CC   DDC CC.BD   CC hukum rajai chalna, naanak likhiya   naali

5.   HAM MAILE TUM UJAL KARTE

Film: Naanak Naam Jahaaz hai (1969)   Music: S. Mohinder
Sabad   Singer: Manna Dey
Taal: Kaharwa   Chord: CE^{b}G S=C#
Transpose+1 and play from C Scale
sorathi mahala 5 (bani guru arjun dev ji)

ham maile tum ujal karte ham nirgun tu data
ham murakh tum chatur siyane tu sarb kalaa ka giyata

madho ham aise tu aisa
ham paapi tum paap khandan neeko thakur desa

tum sabh saaje saaji nivaje jeeu pindu de prana
nirguni aare gunu nahin koii tum daanu dehu miharbana

tum karahu bhala ham bhalo na jaanah tum sadaa sadaa daiyala
tum sukhdaayi purakh bidhate tum raakhahu apune baala

tum nidhan atal sulitaan jiiv jant sabhi jaachai
kahu naanak ham ihai havaala raakhu santan kai paachai

Vinod Kumar

HAM MAILE TUM UJAL KARTE

dhage	nti	nke	dhin	dhage	nti	nke	dhin	dhage	nti	nke dhin	dhage	nti	nke	dhin
12	34	56	78	12	34	56	78	12	34	56 78	12	34	56	78

$D^{b'}D^{b'}$ $D^{b'}D^{b'}$ $D^{b'}D^{b'}$ $C'D^{b'}F'$ $D^{b'}C'$ $C'C'C'$
ham maile tum   u--------jal   karte

$C'D^{b'}$ $C'B^{b}B^{b}B^{b}$ $B^{b}A$ $B^{b}D^{b'}C'$
ham   nirgun   tu   data

$C'D^{b'}$ $C'B^{b}B^{b}B^{b}$ $B^{b}B^{b}$ $B^{b}C'B^{b}C'$ $B^{b}AGF$
ham   murakh   tum   chatur   siyane

F GF $E^{b}D^{b}.B^{b}$ $E^{b}D^{b}$ C-C-
tu sarb kalaa   ka   giyata

F FAA AB^{b} $B^{b}E^{b'}$ $D^{b'}$ $D^{b'}C'$ ---- $C'D^{b'}E^{b'}$
tu sarb kalaa ka   giyata

$D^{b'}C'B^{b}AGF$ GF $E^{b}D^{b}C.B^{b}$ $E^{b}D^{b}$ CC
ma-dho--- ham aise   tu aisa

F	-	G	F	-	GF	E^{b}	D^{b}	C	$.B^{b}$	$E^{b}D^{b}$	C	-	C	-
ma	-	dho	-	-	hm	ae	-	se	-	tu -	ae	-	sa	-
F	A	B^{b}	$D^{b'}$	C'	-	$B^{b}C'$	A	-	B^{b}	A G	F	F	F	-
h	m	pa	-	pi	-	tu-	m	-	pa	- p	khn	d	n	-
$D^{b'}$	-	$D^{b'}$	-	$D^{b'}$	F'	$D^{b'}$	C'	C'	-	C' -	$E^{b'}$	$D^{b'}$	C'	$B^{b}A$
ni	-	ko	-	tha	-	ku	r	de	-	sa -	ma	-	dho	-
GF	GF	E^{b}	D^{b}	C	$.B^{b}$	E^{b}	D^{b}	C	-	C -	-	-	-	-
-	hm	ae	-	se	-	tu	-	ae	-	sa -	-	-	-	-

interlude: F A B^{b} C' - - - C' $D^{b'}$ C' $D^{b'}$ B^{b} C' $B^{b}C'$ – A- F
            G F E^{b} D^{b} C $.B^{b}$ E^{b} D^{b} C – C - - - -

-	FE	C	D^{b}	E	-	F	-	F	E	C D^{b}	E	-	F	-
-	tum	s	b	sa	-	je	-	sa	-	j ni	va	-	je	-

- A B♭ C'	B♭ C' A G	F - F -	- - - -
- ji a p	nu d de -	pra - na -	- - - -

music: C'D♭' ---- C'D♭'C'B♭ AGF---

- AA B♭ C'	C' - B♭ C'	A AA G G	F - F -
- nir gu n	aa - re -	- gun n hi	ko - ii -

- D♭'D♭' D♭' -	D♭' D♭' C'D♭'D♭'F'	D♭' D♭'C'C' -	C' - D♭' E♭'
- tum da -	n de yo -	me hr ba -	na - - -

E♭' D♭' C' B♭A	GF GF E♭ D♭	C .B♭ E♭ D♭	C - C -
ma - dho -	- hm ae -	se - tu -	ae - sa -

F G A B♭	- A G F	G F - -	- - E♭ D♭
ma - - -	- dho - -	h m - -	- - ae -

C .B♭ E♭ D♭	C - C -
se - tu -	ae - sa -

Vinod Kumar

6. HE GOVIND HE GOPAL

Sabad Guru Arjundev ji

Singer: Jagjit Singh

Taal: Daadra

Chord: CEG   S=C#

Transpose+1 and play from C Scale

https://youtu.be/6uxVaiNrb4o

he govind he gopal he govind he gopal
he dayaal laal

praan naath anaath sakhe, deen dard nivaar
he govind he gopal

he samrath agamy puran, moh maya dhaar
he govind he gopal

andh kuup mahaa bhayaanak, naanak paar utaar
he govind he gopal

HE GOVIND HE GOPAL

dha	tin	tin	tata	dhin	dhin	dha	tin	tin	tata	dhin	dhin
1	2	3	4	5	6	1	2	3	4	5	6
E	-	-D	E	-	C	D	-	-D	ED	D	C
he	-	-go	vin	-	d	he	-	-go	pa-	-	l
E	-	-E	D	-	-D	C	-	-	-	-	-
he	-	-d	ya	-	-l	la	-	-	-	-	l
E	-	-D	E	-	C	D	-	-D	ED	-	C
he	-	-go	vin	-	d	he	-	-go	pa-	-	l
ED	E	-D	C	.A	DC	C	-	-	-	-	-
he-	-	-d	ya	-	-l	la	-	-	-	-	l
G	-	-G	G	-	G,G	A	-	A	A	G	E
pra	-	-n	na	-	th,a	na	-	th	s	khe	-

G	-	-G	GE	A	E,G	AG	A	A	A	E	G
pra	-	-n	na-	-	th,a	na-	-	th	s	khe	-
C'	-	-C'	G	-G	G	ED	E	-	D	C	-
di	-	-n	d	-rd	ni	va-	-	-	-	r	-
C'	-	-B	C'	-	A	B	-	-A	B	A	G
he	-	-go	vin	-	d	he	-	-go	pa	-	l
G	-	-G	E	-	-D	C	-	-	-	-	-
he	-	-d	ya	-	-l	la	-	-	-	-	l
GE	E	E	G	A	-G	C'	-	-B	D'	C'	C'
he-	s	m	r	th	-a	g	-	-mya	pu	r	n
C'	-	-C'	A	G	-	ED	E	-	D	C	-
mo	-	-h	ma	ya	-	dha-	-	-	-	-	r
G	-	-E	G	A	-A	C'	-	-B	D'	C'	C'
an	-	-dh	ku	p	-m	ha	-	-bh	ya	-	n
C'	-C'	C'	A	-G	-G	ED	E	-	D	C	-
na	-n	k	pa	-r	-u	ta-	-	-	-	-	r

Vinod Kumar

7. JISKE SIR UPAR TU SWAMI

Film: Man Jeete Jag Jeete (1982)   Music : S. Mohinder
Lyrics: Sabad Gurubani   Singer: Md. Rafi
Taal: Kaharwa   Chord: DFA   S=C#
Transpose+1 and play from C Scale
https://youtu.be/hq7uvpO1Xn0

jiske sir upar tu swami so dukh kaisa paave
bol na jane maaya madmaata, marna chitt na aave,

mere ram raaye tu santa ka, sant tere
tere sewak ko bhao kich naahi jamm nahi aave nede,
jiske sir upar tu swami so dukh kaisa paave

jo tere rang raate swami tin ka janam-maran dukh naasa
teri bakhsh na mete koi, satgur ka dilaasa
jiske sir upar tu swami so dukh kaisa paave

naam dhyaayan sukh phal paayan, aath pehar araadhe
teri sharan tere parwaase panch dusht le saadhe,
jiske sir upar tu swami so dukh kaisa paave

gyaan dhyaan kich karm na jaana, saar na jaana teri
sab te waddaa satgur nanak jin kal raakhi meri
jiske sir upar tu swami so dukh kaisa paave

JISKE SIR UPAR TU SWAMI

dha	ge	n	ti	n	ke	dhi	n	dha	ge	n	ti	n	ke	dhi	n
1	2	3	4	5	6	7	8	1	2	3	4	5	6	7	8
	E	E	E	E	D	E	A	G	F	F	G	E	-	D	-
	ji	s	ke	si	r	u	-	p	r	tu	-	swa	-	mi	-
-	E	G	G	A	-	A	D'	C'	B^b	B^b	C'	C'	A	-	-
-	so	du	kh	kai	-	sa	-	pa	-	-	-	ve	-	-	-
A	-	F'	F'	E'	E'	D'	-	B^b	-	C'	D'	D'	-	D'	-
bo	-	l	n	ja	ne	ma	-	ya	-	m	d	ma	-	ta	-
-	C'	C'	C'	B	-	A	G	E	G	A	C'	B^b	-	-	-
-	m	r	na	chi	-	t	n	aa	-	ve	-	-	-	-	-
-	E	E	G	A	-	A	D'	B^b	-	A	-	F	G	E	D
-	m	r	na	chi	-	t	n	aa	-	ve	-	-	-	-	-
-	E	E	E	E	D	E	A	G	F	F	G	E	-	D	-
-	ji	s	ke	si	r	u	-	p	r	tu	-	swa	-	mi	-
-	E	G	G	A	-	A	D'	C'	B^b	B^b	C'	C'	A	-	-
-	so	du	kh	kai	-	sa	-	pa	-	-	-	ve	-	-	-
C	C	D	-	-	-	-	-	C	C	D	-	-	-	-	-
s	t	na	-m	-	-	-	-	s	t	na	-m	-	-	-	-
G-	GG	A-	-	-	-	-	-	G-	GG	A-	-	-	-	F'-	F'E'
va	he,gu	ru	-	-	-	-	-	va	he,gu	ru	-	-	-	va	he,gu
D'-	-	-	-	-	-	D	C	C	-D	D	E	-	-	-	-
ru	-	-	-	-	-	me	re	ra	-m	ra	ye	-	-	-	-

Vinod Kumar

-	G	-	G	F	F	E	E	D	-	D	-	-	-	-	-
-	tu	-	sn	ta	ka	sn	t	te	-	re	-	-	-	-	-
-	G	G	G	A	A	C'	-	-	G	F	F	E	-	D	-
-	te	re	se	v	k	ko	-	-	bhy	ku	chh	na	-	hi	-
-	F	F	F	G	-	E	-	D	-	D	-	-	-	-	-
-	jm	n	hi	aa	-	ve	-	ne	-	re	-	-	-	-	-
-	A	-	A	D'	-	D'	D'	D'E'	F'	E'	D'	C'	-	AB	G
-	jo	-	te	re	-	rn	g	ra-	-	te	-	swa	-	mi	-
-	E	E	E	G	G	G	G	A	A	A	D'	B♭	-	A	-
-	ti	n	ka	j	n	m	m	r	n	du	kh	na	-	sa	-
A	-	F'	-	E'	-	D'	D'	B♭	-	D'	-	D'	-	D'	-
te	-	ri	-	b	k	sh	n	me	-	te	-	ko	-	ii	-
-	C'	C'	B	A	B	G	G	E	G	A	C'	B♭	-	-	-
-	st	gu	ru	ka	-	-	di	la	-	sa	-	-	-	-	-
-	EE	G	G	A	G	A	D'	B♭	-	A	-	F	G	E	D
-	st	gu	ru	ka	-	-	di	la	-	sa	-	-	-	-	-
-	E	E	E	E	D	E	A	G	F	F	G	E	-	D	-
-	ji	s	ke	si	r	u	-	p	r	tu	-	swa	-	mi	-
-	E	G	G	A	-	A	D'	C'	B♭	B♭	C'	C'	A	-	-
-	so	du	kh	kai	-	sa	-	pa	-	-	-	ve	-	-	-
C	C	D	-	-	-	-	-	C	C	D	-	-	-	-	-
s	t	na	-m	-	-	-	-	s	t	na	-m	-	-	-	-
G	GG	A	-	-	-	-	-	G	GG	A	-	-	-	F'	F'E'
va	he,gu	ru	-	-	-	-	-	va	he,gu	ru	-	-	-	va	he,gu

D'	-	-	-	-	-	-	-								
ru	-	-	-	-	-	-	-								
C	-C	D	E	-	-	-	-	D	C	D	E	-	-	-	-
na	m,dh	ya	yn	-	-	-	-	sukh	fl	pa	yn	-	-	-	-
G	-	F	F	G	F	E	-	D	-	D	-	-	-	-	-
aa	-	th	p	h	r	aa	-	ra	-	dhe	-	-	-	-	-
-	G	-	G	A	A	A	A	C'	-	G	F	E	-	D	-
-	te	-	ri	sh	r	n	te	re	-	p	r	va	h	se	-
-	F	F	G	-	F	E	-	D	-	D	-	-	-	-	-
-	pn	ch	du	-	sht	lai	-	sa	-	de	-	-	-	-	-
-	A	A	A	D'	D'	D'	D'	D'E'	F'	E'	D'	C'	-	AB	G
-	gya	n	dhya	-	n	ku	chh	k	r	m	n	ja	-	na-	-
-	E	G	G	A	-	A	D'	B♭	-	A	-	-	-	-	-
-	sa	r	na	ja	-	na	-	te	-	ri	-	-	-	-	-
-	A	A	F'	E'	-	D'	-	C'	B♭	C'	D'	D'	-	D'	D'
-	s	b	te	v	d	da	-	s	t	gu	ru	na	-	n	k
C'	C'	C'	C'	B	-	A	G	E	G	A	C'	B♭	-	-	-
ji	n	k	l	ra	-	khii	-	me	-	ri	-	-	-	-	-
E	E	G	G	A	-	A	D'	B♭	-	A	-	F	G	E	D
ji	n	k	l	ra	-	khii	-	me	-	ri	-	-	-	-	-
-	E	E	E	E	D	E	A	G	F	F	G	E	-	D	-
-	ji	s	ke	si	r	u	-	p	r	tu	-	swa	-	mi	-

Vinod Kumar

-	E	G	G	A	-	A	D'	C'	B♭	B♭	C'	C'	A	-	-
-	so	du	kh	kai	-	sa	-	pa	-	-	-	ve	-	-	-
C	C	D	-	-	-	-	-	C	C	D	-	-	-	-	-
s	t	na	-m	-	-	-	-	s	t	na	-m	-	-	-	-
G	GG	A	-	-	-	-	-	G	GG	A	-	-	-	F'	F'E'
va	he,gu	ru	-	-	-	-	-	va	he,gu	ru	-	-	-	va	he,gu
D'	-	-	-	-	-	-	-								
ru	-	-	-	-	-	-	-								

8.   JO MANGE THAKUR APNE TE

World gurudwara.com   Chord: GBD'   S=C#

Sabad Gurubani Taal:
Kaharwa   Transpose+1 and play from C Scale

https://www.youtube.com/watch?v=jkfvNRnYehk

jo mange thakur apne te soi soi deve
nanak das mukh te jo bole eeha uha such hovay
jo mange thakur apne te soi soi deve

chatur disa kino bal apna, sir upar kar dhareyo
kirpa katakh avalokan kino, das ka dukh bidaryo
jo mange thakur apne te soi soi deve

hari jan raakhe gur govind rakhe gur govind
kanth lae avguna sab mete, dyal purakh bakshind
jo mange thakur apne te soi soi deve

JO MANGE THAKUR APNE TE

dha	tit	tin	tin	ta	tit	dhin	dhin	dha	tit	tin	tin	ta	tit	dhin	dhin
1	2	3	4	5	6	7	8	1	2	3	4	5	6	7	8
	B	-	B	B	-	B	A	G	A	A	A	G	F$^{\#}$	E	D
	jo	-	man	ge	-	tha	-	ku	r	a	p	ne	-	te	-
-	E	G	G	A	G	A	B	A	G	G	-	-	-	-	-
-	so	-	i	so	-	ii	-	de	-	vai	-	-	-	-	-
-	D'	D'	D'	D'	-D'	D'	D'	D'	E'	E'	D'	D'	C'	C'	-
-	na	n	k	da	-s	mu	kh	te	-	jo	-	bo	-	le	-
C'	D'	-	C'	B	-	A	G	G	A	A	B	-	-	-	-
i	ha	-	u	ha	-	s	ch	ho	-	vai	-	-	-	-	-
-	D'	D'	D'	D'	-D'	D'	D'	D'	E'	E'	D'	D'	C'	C'	-
-	chtu	r	di	sa	-	kii	-	nho	-	b	l	a	p	na	-
-	C'	D'	C'	B	A	A	G	G	A	A	B	-	-	-	-
-	si	r	u	p	r	k	r	dha	r	yo	-	-	-	-	-
-	D'	D'	D'	D'	-D'	D'	D'	D'	E'	E'	D'	D'	C'	C'	-
-	kir	pa	k	ta	khu	a	v	lo	-	k	n	kii	-	nyo	-
-	C'	D'	C'	B	-	A	G	G	A	A	B	-	-	-	-
-	da	s	ka	du	-	kh	vi	da	r	yo	-	-	-	-	-
-	D'	D'	D'	D'	-	D'	-	D'	E'	E'	D'	D'	C'	C'	-
-	hri	j	n	ra	-	khe	-	gu	r	go	-	vin	-	d	-
-	C'	D'	C'	B	B	A	G	G	A	A	B	-	-	-	-
-	ra	-	khe	gu	r	go	-	vin	-	d	-	-	-	-	-
-	D'	D'	D'	D'	-	D'	D'	D'	E'	E'	D'	D'	C'	C'	-
-	kn	th	la	ye	-	a	v	gu	n	s	b	me	-	te	-
C'	D'	D'	C'	B	B	A	G	G	A	A	B	-	-	-	-
d	ya	l	pu	r	kh	b	k	shin	-	d	-	-	-	-	-

Vinod Kumar

-	B	-	B	B	-	B	A	G	A	A	A	G	F$^\#$	E	D
-	jo	-	man	ge	-	tha	-	ku	r	a	p	ne	-	te	-
-	E	G	G	A	G	A	B	A	G	G	-	-	-	-	-
-	so	-	i	so	-	ii	-	de	-	vai	-	-	-	-	-

9. KIRPA KARO DEEN KE DAATE

Sabad, Mahla 5 Ghar 1   Singer: Bhai Kavaldeep Singh ji
Taal: Kaharwa   Chord: DF$^\#$A   S=C#
Transpose+1 and play from C Scale
https://youtu.be/mq8LLPRZwVE

kirpa karo deen ke date mera gun avgan na bicharo koi.

mati ka kiya dope suami, manas ki gat ayhi. ||1||

mere man satgur sev sukh hoyi.

jo ichahu soyi fal pavoh fir dukh na viape koi. ||1|| rahaa-o.

kache bhande saji nivaje antar jot samahi.

jaisa likhat likhiya dhuri karte ham taesi kirat kamai. ||2||

man tan thapi kiya sab apna eho avan jaana.

 jin diya so chit na aawey mohi andh laptana. ||3||

jin kiya soyi prab jaane har ka mahal apara.

bhagat kari har ke gun gavan nanak das tumara. ||4||1||

KIRPA KARO DEEN KE DAATE

dha	ge	n	ti	n	ke	dhi	n	dha	ge	n	ti	n	ke	dhi	n
1	2	3	4	5	6	7	8	1	2	3	4	5	6	7	8

ED   EF$^\#$ F$^\#$E   F$^\#$AG
kirpa   kro   kirpa   kro-

 GA   AB GEF$^\#$ D   EE
kirpa   kro di-n   ke date

F$^\#$F$^\#$ F$^\#$G EECD .B CEEE F$^\#$F$^\#$
mera gun   avgun   n vicharo koii

GAG F$^\#$G EECD .B CEEE DGF$^\#$E
me-ra gun   avgun n vicharo o-----

AB   D'C'D'B A   AB   D'C'D'B
mati ka   kiya thopai suaami

BB   GA F$^\#$F$^\#$ EE BB   GA F$^\#$F$^\#$ ECD.B
mans kii gti   ehi mans kii gti   ehi

AB   D'C'D'B E'E'E'E' E'D' F$^\#$E' C'D'E'
mere mn---   stiguru sev sukh ho-ii

A BD'C'D'B A   B D'C'D'B E' E'E' E' E'D'F$^\#$E' C'D'E'
jo ichchhahu soii fal pavhu fir dukh n viyape   koii

B BC'B A F$^\#$AGF$^\#$ EE B BC'B   A F$^\#$AGF$^\#$ ECD.B
fir du-kh n viya-pe koii fir du-kh n viyape ko---ii-

AB   D'C'D'B   AB D'C'D'B E'E' E'D'F$^{\#'}$ E'C'D'E'
kache bhan---de saji niva-je antr jo-t   sma-ii

AB   D'C'D'B AAA   BB D'C'D'B E' E'E' E'D'F$^{\#'}$ E'C'D'E'
jaisa likh-t   likhiya dhuri kr-tai   hm aesi kirt   kma-ii

B   BA F$^\#$F$^\#$AG   F$^\#$E E B BA F$^\#$F$^\#$AG F$^\#$E CD.B
hm aesi kirt-   kma-ii hm aesi kirt-   kma-ii---

Vinod Kumar

A   B   D'C'D'B   AA   BB   D'C'D'B   E'E'   E'D'F#'E'   C'D'E'
mn tn tha--pi   kiya sbh ap-na   eho   aa-vn   ja-na

 A   BD'C'D'B   A   AB B   D'C'D'B   E'E'   E'D'   F#'E'C'D'E'
jin   diya-----   so chit n aa---vai mohi andh lipta-na

BA   F#A GF# E E BA   F#A GF# E CD.B
mohi andh lipta-na   mohi andh lipta-na---

A BD'C'D'B   A   BB   D'C'D'B E' E' E'D'F#'   E'C'D'E'
jin kiya----   soii prbh ja-ne- hri ka mhl   apa-ra

AAB B D'C'D'B A A   B   D'C'D'B E'E'E' E'D'F#'   E'C'D'E'
bhgti kri-----   hri ke gun ga-va- nank   da-s   tumhara

BAG F#AG F#EE   BAG F#AG F#ECD.B
nank das   tumhara nank das   tumhara

10. KYA TU SOYA JAAG IYANA

Taal: Roopak   Chord: EGB   S=C#

Transpose+1 and play from C Scale

Bhai Maninder Singh Ji (Sri Nagar Wale)

https://youtu.be/U9Oq8zQlhrs

kya tu soya jag eyana tai jeevan jag sach kar jaana

jo din aavay so din jaahee karna kooch rahan er naahin
sang chalat hain ham bhee chalna door gavan sir uupar marna
kya tu soya ----

jin jio deeya so rizak ambraaye sab ghar bheetar haat chalaaye
kar bandagee chhad main mera hirday naam smaari savera
kya tu soya ----

janam siraana ant na sanvaara saanjh pari dah disi andhiyaara
kah ravidas nidani deewane chetas naahin duniya bhankhaane
kya tu soya ----

Vinod Kumar

KYA TU SOYA JAAG IYANA

dha 1	dhi 2	na 3	dha 4	ti 5	dha 6	ti 7	dha 1	dhi 2	na 3	dha 4	ti 5	dha 6	ti 7
B	-	-	A	B	$D^{b'}$	-	A	-	-	A^b	-	E	-
kya	-	-	tu	-	-	-	so	-	-	ya	-	-	-
E	-	-	$F^{\#}$	-	-	B	G	$F^{\#}$	-	G	-	E	-
ja	-	-	g	-	-	i	ya	-	-	na	-	-	-
B	-	-	A	B	$D^{b'}$	-	A	-	-	A^b	-	E	-
tai	-	-	ji	-	-	-	vn	-	-	j	-	g	-
E	E	-	$F^{\#}$	-	B	-	G	$F^{\#}$	-	G	-	E	-
s	ch	-	k	-	r	-	ja	-	-	na	-	-	-

interlude: (EGB) $D^{b'}$BABD$^{b'}$---- A $D^{b'}$ A $D^{b'}$ B G B A G,

G- E EAGF$^{\#}$E

B – $D^{b'}$ – D' – $D^{b'}$ –$D^{b'}$ B,   G E- G- B- $D^{b'}$- BB

dha 1	dhi 2	na 3	dha 4	ti 5	dha 6	ti 7	dha 1	dhi 2	na 3	dha 4	ti 5	dha 6	ti 7
$D^{b'}$	-	-	$D^{b'}$	-	$D^{b'}$	-	D'	-	-	B	-	-	-
jo	-	-	di	-	n	-	aa	-	-	ve	-	-	-
G	E	-	G	-	B	-	$D^{b'}$	-	-	B	-	-	-
so	-	-	di	-	n	-	ja	-	-	hi	-	-	-
$D^{b'}$	$D^{b'}$	-	$D^{b'}$	-	-	-	E'	-	D'	B	-	-	G
k	r	-	na	-	-	-	ku	-	-	ch	-	-	r
G	E	-	G	-	B	-	$D^{b'}$	-	-	B	-	-	-
h	n	-	ae	-	r	-	na	-	-	hi	-	-	-
B	-	-	$D^{b'}$	D'	B	$D^{b'}$	D'	$F^{\#'}$	-	E'	-	-	-
sn	-	-	g	-	-	ch	l	t	-	hai	-	-	-
B	-	-	$D^{b'}$	D'	-	-	$D^{b'}$	-	-	B	-	-	-
hm	-	-	bhi	-	-	-	chl	-	-	na	-	-	-
B	-	-	$D^{b'}$	D'	B	$D^{b'}$	D'	$F^{\#'}$	E'	E'	-	B	B
du	-	-	r	-	-	g	v	n	-	-	-	si	r

B - - | Db' - | D' - | Db' Db' - | B - | - -
u - - | p - | r - | m r - | na - | - -

B - - | A B | Db' Db' | A Ab - | - - | E E
du - - | r - | - g | v n - | - - | si r

E - - | F# - | B - | G F# - | G - | E -
u - - | p - | r - | m r - | na - | - -

B - - | A B | Db' - | A - - | Ab - | E -
kya - - | tu - | - - | so - - | ya - | - -

E - - | F# - | - B | G - F# | G - | E -
ja - - | g - | - i | ya - - | na - | - -

interlude: (EGB) Db'BABDb'---- A Db' A Db' B G B A G,
                    G- E EAGF#E
                    B – Db' – D' – Db' –Db' B,   G E- G- B- Db'- BB

Db' Db' - | Db' - | Db' - | D' - - | B - | B -
ji n - | ji - | o - | di - - | aa - | so -

G E - | G - | B B | Db' - - | B - | - -
ri j - | k - | am b | ra - - | e - | - -

Db' Db' - | Db' - | Db' - | D' - - | B - | B -
s b - | gh - | t - | bhi - - | t - | r -

G E - | G - | - B | Db' B - | B - | - -
ha - - | t - | - ch | la - - | e - | - -

B B - | Db' D' | B Db' | D' F#' E' | E' - | - -
k r - | bn - | - d | gi - - | - - | - -

B - B | Db' D' | - - | Db' - - | B - | - -
chh - d | mai - | - - | me - - | ra - | - -

B B - | Db' D' | B Db' | D' F#' E' | E' - | - B
hi r - | dai - | - - | na - - | m - | - s

Vinod Kumar

```
B   -   -   | Db'  D'  -   D'  | Db'  -   -   | B   -   | -   -
ma  -   -   | r    -   -   s   | ve   -   -   | ra  -   | -   -

B   B   -   | A    B   Db' B   | A    -   -   | Ab  -   | -   E
hi  r   -   | dai  -   -   -   | na   -   -   | m   -   | -   s

E   -   -   | F#   -   -   B   | G    F#  -   | G   -   | E   -
ma  -   -   | r    -   -   s   | ve   -   -   | ra  -   | -   -

B   -   -   | A    B   Db' -   | A    -   -   | Ab  -   | E   -
kya -   -   | tu   -   -   -   | so   -   -   | ya  -   | -   -

E   -   -   | F#   -   -   B   | G    F#  -   | G   -   | E   -
ja  -   -   | g    -   -   i   | ya   -   -   | na  -   | -   -
```

interlude: (EGB) Db'BABDb'---- A Db' A Db' B G B A G,

        G- E EAGF#E

        B – Db' – D' – Db' –Db' B,   G E- G- B- Db'- BB

```
Db' Db' -   | Db'  -   -   Db' | D'   -   -   | B   -   | -   -
j   n   -   | m    -   -   si  | ra   -   -   | no  -   | -   -

G   -   E   | G    -   -   B   | Db'  -   -   | B   -   | -   -
an  -   t   | na   -   -   s   | va   -   -   | ra  -   | -   -

Db' -   -   | Db'  -   -   Db' | D'   E'  D'  | B   -   | B   B
san -   -   | jh   -   -   p   | ri   -   -   | -   -   | d   h

G   E   -   | -    -   G   B   | Db'  B   -   | B   -   | -   -
di  s   -   | -    -   an  dhi | ya   -   -   | ra  -   | -   -

B   B   -   | Db'  -   B   Db' | D'   F#' E'  | E'  -   | -   B
k   h   -   | -    -   r   vi  | da   -   -   | s   -   | -   ni

B   -   -   | Db'  D'  -   D'  | Db'  -   -   | B   -   | -   -
da  -   -   | n    -   -   di  | va   -   -   | ne  -   | -   -

B   -   -   | Db'  D'  B   Db' | D'   F#' E'  | E'  -   | -   B
che -   -   | t    -   s   -   | na   -   -   | hi  -   | -   duni

B   -   -   | Db'  -   D'  D'  | Db'  -   -   | B   -   | -   -
ya  -   -   | -    -   a   n   | kha  -   -   | ne  -   | -   -
```

B	-	-	A	B	D$^{b'}$	B	A	-	-	A^{b}	-	-	E
che	-	-	t	-	-	s	na	-	-	hi	-	-	duni
E	-	-	F$^{\#}$	-	B	B	G	F$^{\#}$	-	G	-	E	-
ya	-	-	-	-	a	n	kha	-	-	ne	-	-	-
B	-	-	A	B	D$^{b'}$	-	A	-	-	A^{b}	-	E	-
kya	-	-	tu	-	-	-	so	-	-	ya	-	-	-
E	-	-	F$^{\#}$	-	-	B	G	-	F$^{\#}$	G	-	E	-
ja	-	-	g	-	-	i	ya	-	-	na	-	-	-

11. MAI MAIN DHAN PAYO HARI NAM

Sabad Guru Teg Bahadur Ji
Taal: Kaharwa
Transpose+1 and play from C Scale

Singer: Bhai Sohan Singh
Rasia
Chord: DFA GB^{b}D'   S=C#

https://youtu.be/5cinYoKuLVU Nupur Audio

basantu mahla 9

maee main dhan paiyo har naamu
manu mero dhaawan te chhutio kari baitho bisraam

maaiya mamta tan te bhaagi upajio nirmal giyanu
lobh moh eh parasi n saakai gahi bhagati bhagwaan

janam janam ka sansa chuka ratanu naamu jab paaiyaa
trisna sakal binasi man te nij sukh maahi samaaiya

ja kau hot daiyalu kirpa nidhi so govind gun gavai
kahu naanak ih bidhi ki sampai kou gurmukhi paavai

Vinod Kumar

MAI MAIN DHAN PAYO HARI NAM

dha	ge	n	ti	n	ke	dhi	n	dha	ge	n	ti	n	ke	dhi	n
1	2	3	4	5	6	7	8	1	2	3	4	5	6	7	8

```
DE   DC    E    EFGF  ED   D-
maii mai-  dhnu paio- hri  namu

DEG  EDC   EE   EFGF  ED   D-
maii- mai- -    dhnu  paio- hri  namu

AG   GFE   EFGF E  DDD   BB BC’D’C’   BAA-
mnu  me-ro dha-vn te chhutio kri bai-tho-   bisramu

EE   EFGF   EDD-
kri  bai-tho-  bisramu

interlude: sitar :
DEF- FDE- DC.Bᵇ- FED-
DEF- EFG- FGA- AGA- GFG-E
AA-G  FG-G  A—

G A    C’BᵇC’A GG A C’BᵇC’A D’ D’  D’ D’  BᵇBᵇC’E’ D’---
maiaa  mmta-     tn te bha-gi- upjio  nirml  giaanu

D’ D’  D’ D’   BᵇC’E’D’  D’---
upjio  nirml   giaanu

G G A A  GGC’A   F-- EGD
upjio       nirml  giaa--nu

GA   C’Bᵇ C’A  GGA A  C’BᵇC’A  D’D’  BᵇC’C’  E’D’D’-
lobh moh eh    prsi n sa-kai-  ghi   bhgti   bhgvan

AA  GGG  AAF--EGD
ghi bhgti  bhgva---- n

GGA AC’Bᵇ C’A GA   C’BᵇC’A  D’D’D’  D’BᵇC’  E’D’   D’ D’
jnm jnm  ka- snsa chu-ka-   rtnu    na-mu   jb     paiaa

GGA AGA    C’A F---EGD
rtnu na-mu jb  pa—iaa-
```

```
GGA   C'B♭C'A  GGA   C'B♭ C'A  D'D'  D'D'  B♭C'E'  D'  D'  D'
trisna  skl-         binasi  mn  te-  nij  sukh  ma-hi   smaiaa

GG   AA   AGC'  AF – EGD
nij   sukh  ma-hi  sma—iaa-

G  A  C'B♭C'A  G GA  A  C'B♭  C'A   D'  D'B♭C'  E'D'  D'D'
ja  ku  ho-t-       diaalu  kir pa-  nidhi  so  gobind  gun  gavai

G   AC'B♭  C'A  GG   A  C'B♭C'A   D'D'  B♭C'E'D'  D'D'
khu  nank   ih  bidhi  kii  sn—pai--  kou  gurmukhi  pavai

 GA  GAC'A   F—EGD
kou  gurmukhi  pa----vai-
```

12. MAIN ANDHULE KI TEK

Sabad Naamdev Ji
Taal: Daadra
Transpose+1 and play from C Scale
https://youtu.be/l-hxhcQYd9Y

Singer: Bhai Harjinder Singh Shri
Nagar wale
Chord: DFA   S=C#

main andhule ki tek tera naam khundkara

main gareeb main maskeen, tera naam hai aadhaara

kareema raheema, allah tu gani

haazraa huzur, dar pesh tu mani, dar pesh tu mani

dariyav tu dihand tu, bisi aar tu dhani

dehi lehi ek tu, digar ko nahin, digar ko nahin

tu daana tu beena, main bichaar kya kari

name che swami, bakshand tu hari, bakshand tu hari

Vinod Kumar

MAIN ANDHULE KI TEK

dha	dhi	na	dha	tu	na	dha	dhi	na	dha	tu	na
1	2	3	4	5	6	1	2	3	4	5	6

AAF' D'   D'D'E'D'C'B^{b}C'A
digr   ko   nhi

AG   AGA GFDEED
digr   ko   nhi

A GAB^{b}A   B^b D'C'E'D'
tu dana   tu   bina

AF'E'F'E'   D'D'D' E'D'   C'B^{b}C'A
mai   bichar kya   kari

GAB^{b}A B^b D'C'E'D'
name   che   swami

AAAF'E'F'E'D'   D'   D'E'D'C'B^{b}C'A
bkshnd   tu   hari

AAGG   AGA GFDEED
bkshnd   tu   hari

Vinod Kumar

13. MERE SAHIB MERE SAHIB

Film: Naanak Naam Jahaaz hai (1969)   Music: S. Mohinder
Sabad   Singer: Asha Bhonsle
Taal: Daadra   Chord: CEG   S=D
Transpose+2 and play from C Scale
https://www.youtube.com/watch?v=_QIqyhWHP6s

mahla 5 ghar 7 (bani guru arjun dev ji)
aa……………..
mere saahib mere saahib, tu main maan nimaani
ardaas kari prabh apne aage, suni suni jeevaan teri baani

tudhu chiti aaye maha aananda, jisu bisrahi so mari jaaye
daiyalu hovahi jisu upari karte, so tudhu sadaa dhiyaye

charan dhuuli tere jan ki hovan, tere darsan kau bali jaaee
amrit bachan ridai uri dhaari, tau kirpa te sangu paaee

antar ki gati tudhu pahi saari, tudhu jevadu avaru na koee
jis nu laai lehi so laage, bhagatu tuhara soee

dui kar jori maangau iku dana, sahib tutthe paavaan
saansi saansi naanaku aaraadhai, aath pahar gun gaavaan

MERE SAHIB MERE SAHIB

dha	dhi	na	dha	tu	na	dha	dhi	na	dha	tu	na
1	2	3	4	5	6	1	2	3	4	5	6

G-G C'B D'C' G A- G F-
aa----------------------

FA--- B A G E F G – D E – D C –
aa--------------------------------

CD   FEE CD   .BCC
mere sahib mere   sahib

G   A   F   D DEF   E   E   G   F   C EDD C
tu mai man ni ma-ni tu mai man ni ma—ni

GAC'-G AC' E   EEE DDC
ardasi kri   prbh apne aage-

 E   EE GG AB GAG
suni suni jiva teri bani

 DD DD EE GG FE-D-C
suni suni jiva teri bani-----

CD   FEE CD .BCC
mere sahib mere sahib

C'C'   GA C'C' EE GDDC
tudhu   chiti aae mha aannda-

 E   EE G AB GAG
jisu visrhi so mri jae

AC'G   AC'   E EEG D DC
diaalu hovhi jisu upri   krte-

E EE   GA   B G AG-ED
so tudhu sda dhiaae------

Vinod Kumar

```
 D   DD    EF  GFE-DC
so  tudhu sda  dhiaae----

CD     FEE   CD      .BCC
mere  sahib mere    sahib

C'C'  C'C'     C'C'  B  A  AB-AG
chrn  dhuli    tere jan kii hova---

GG   G A   G    F   FG
tere drsn  ku   bali jaii

C'C'   C'C'    C'B  A   AB-AG
amrit bchn  ridai uri dhari----

G   G A   G  F   FG
tu kirpa  te sngu paii

CD      FEE  CD  .BCC
mere   sahib mere sahib

 E'E'   E'   E'E'  D'  D'C'  C'D'-C'B
antr    kii  gti  tudhu phi sari-----

BB       C'C'B AAB  B  C'C'
tudhu  jevdu  avru  n  koii

C'  C'   C'C'  C'B  A  AAB-AG
jis nu  lai   laihi so lage------

GGA    GFF   FG-FED
bhgtu  tuhara soii-----

DDD   DEFG FE-D-C
bhgtu tuhara  soii-----

CD    FEE  CD      .BCC
mere  sahib mere    sahib

C'  GA  C'C'  EE   EG  DD
duii kr  jodi mangu iku dana
```

```
EEE   GAB    GAG
sahib  tuthai-  pava-

C'G     AC'C'    EE   EGDDC
saansi saan-si  nanku  aa-radhe-

EE   EG   AB  GAG- FED
aath phr   gun  gava--------

 DD   DE   GG  FE-D-C
aath phr   gun  gava-----

CD     FEE  CD    .BCC
mere  sahib mere    sahib
```

14. MITR PIYARE NU

Sabad Gurugranth Saaheb   Music: S. Mohinder
Film: Naanak Naam Jahaaz hai (1969)   Singer: Md. Rafi
Taal: Kaharwa   Chord: DGB^b S=C#
Transpose+1 and play from C Scale
https://youtu.be/1zKx_5J-ZHI

mitr piyare nu, haalu mureedaan da kahina

tudhu binu rogu rajaaiyaan da odhan
naag nivaasaan de rahnaa

suul suraahi khanjar piyala
bing kasaaiyaan da sahina

yarade da saanu satthar changa
bhath khediyaan da rahna

Vinod Kumar

MITR PIYARE NU

dha	ge	n	ti	n	ke	dhi	n	dha	ge	n	ti	n	ke	dhi	n
1	2	3	4	5	6	7	8	1	2	3	4	5	6	7	8

DDF G GB♭G F E♭   AA C'C'D'B♭   B♭ G A♭B♭A♭--G —FE♭
mitr piaa--- re nu , halu muri-da   da khi- -----na -----

interlude:
AB♭ AB♭ G A G
GA C'D' D' C'B♭ A G
G'F' E♭'D' C'B♭ AG FB♭
A D' ᴳF E♭

B♭B♭   B♭B♭   AGA   C'C'E♭'E♭' E♭' D'F'E♭'E♭'
tudhu   binu   ro-gu rjaiiaa   da o-dhn,

E♭'G'G' G' F' D' E♭'   F'ᴳ' E♭'-- C'--B♭
na-g   niva-san de   rhna--------

B♭B♭   B♭ B♭D'C'D'B♭   B♭   B♭F GB♭A♭B♭G
nag   ni va----san   de rh—na-----

DDF G GB♭G F E♭   AA   C'C'D'B♭   B♭   G A♭B♭A♭--G —FE♭
mitr piaa--- re nu , halu muri-da   da khi- -----na -----

interlude:
B♭- A- G A G –
DFE DFGAB♭G FGAB♭C'A AC'D'E'F'-- D'F'G'A'B♭'-
D' F' G' A' B♭'-
B♭ F'- F'E♭'D'C'B♭AGF B♭G
GB♭C'D'E♭'-
E♭'E♭' D'C'B♭C'B♭ E♭'E♭'E♭' E♭'B♭C'B♭

E♭'E♭'   D' C'B♭C'B♭   E♭'E♭'E♭'   D'C'B♭C'B♭
sul   sura---hi--   khnjr   piaa-la-,

E♭'E♭'   E♭'E♭'—F' G' F'—E♭' C' B♭
bing   ksaiiaa   da sahina

B^{b}B^b B^{b}B^b D'C'D'   B^b B^b B^{b}F GB^{b}A^{b}B^b G--
bing   ksaii----aa   da shi-na------   mitr piaare nu

interlude:
AB^b AB^b G A G
GA C'D' D' C'B^b A G
G'F' E^b'D' C'B^b AG FB^b
A D' ^{G}F E^b

B^{b}B^{b}B^b AGAG AC'   E^b'E^b'E^b'   D'F'E^b'-C'
yarde   da---- sanu stthr   chn-ga--,

B^{b}B^{b}B^b AGAG AC'   E^b'E^b'E^b'   D'F'E^b'-C'
yarde   da---- sanu stthr   chn-ga--,

E^b'G' G'G'F'   D'E^b'   F'—E^b'---^{D}'C' B^b
bhth khediaa   da   rhna -----

B^{b}B^b B^{b}B^b B^{b}D'C'D'   B^b B^b-F GB^{b}A^b- G
bhth khediaa-   da   rh- na------   mitr piaare nu

Vinod Kumar

15. MU LALAN SAU PREET BANI

Taal: Kaharwa   Chord: E^{b}GB^b S=C#
Transpose+1 and play from C Scale
https://youtu.be/87URm2Ms1EU
Bhai Harjinder Singh ji Shri Nagar Wale

mu lalan siyon preet bani

tori na tutte chhori na chhuttai, aisii madho khinch tani
divas rain man maahi basat hai, tu kar kirpa prabh apni

bal bal jaaun shyam sunder ko, akath kathaa jaaki baat sunii
jan nanak daasan daas kahiyat hai, mohi karahu kirpa thakur apni

MU LALAN SAU PREET BANI

dhin	-	na	dhin	-	na	tin	-	dhin	-	na	dhin	-	na	tin	-
1	2	3	4	5	6	7	8	1	2	3	4	5	6	7	8
	B^b	A	G	G	G	G	-	F	-	-D	E^b	G	-	-	-
	mu	-	la	l	n	so	-	pri	-	-t	b	ni	-	-	-
-	B^b	A	G	G	G	G	-	F	-	-D	E^b	B^b	G	-	-
-	mu	-	la	l	n	so	-	pri	-	-t	b	ni	-	-	-
G	-	-A	B^b	B^b	A	A	G	G	-	-A	B^b	B^b	A	A	G
to	-	-ri	n	tu	-	tai	-	chho	-	-ri	n	chhu	-	te	-
-	G	A	A	G	A	G	F	G	-	-A	A	A	-	-	-
-	ae	-	si	ma	-	dho	-	khin	-	-ch	t	ni	-	-	-

	B♭	A	G	G	G	G	-	F	-	-D	E♭	G	-	-	-
	mu	-	la	l	n	so	-	pri	-	-t	b	ni	-	-	-
-	B♭	A	G	G	G	G	-	F	-	-D	E♭	B♭	G	-	-
-	mu	-	la	l	n	so	-	pri	-	-t	b	ni	-	-	-
D'C'	-E♭'	-	D'	-	D'	C'	B♭	D'C'	-E♭'	-	D'	D'	D'	D'	-
div	-s	-	rai	-	n	m	n	ma-	-hi	-	b	s	t	hai	-
-	D'	-D'	-C'	B♭	A	A	-	G	A	F	G	A	-	-	-
-	tu	-k	-r	ki	r	pa	-	pr	bh	a	p	ni	-	-	-
-	D'	-D'	-C'	B♭	A	G	-	F	G	F	A	G	-	-	-
-	tu	-k	-r	ki	r	pa	-	pr	bh	a	p	ni	-	-	-
D'C'	-E♭'	-	D'	D'	-	C'	B♭	D'C'	-	E♭'	D'	D'	D'	D'	-
bl	-b	-	l	ja	-	un	-	shya	-	m	sun	d	r	ko	-
G	G	D'	C'	B♭	-	A	A	G	A	F	G	A	-	-	-
a	k	th	k	tha	-	ja	kii	ba	-	t	su	ni	-	-	-
G	G	D'	C'	B♭	-	A	A	F	G	F	A	G	-	-	-
a	k	th	k	tha	-	ja	kii	ba	-	t	su	ni	-	-	-
D'C'	-C'	E♭'	D'D'	C'	-	A	B♭	D'	-	C'	C'E♭'	D'	D'	D'	-
jn	-na	-	nk	da	-	s	n	da	-	s	khi	y	t	hai	-
GG	-G	D'	D'C'	B♭	A	G	-	G	A	F	G	A	-	-	-
mohe	-k	ro	kir	pa	-	tha	-	ku	r	a	p	ni	-	-	-
GG	-G	D'	D'C'	B♭	A	G	-	F	G	F	A	G	-	-	-
mohe	-k	ro	kir	pa	-	tha	-	ku	r	a	p	ni	-	-	-

Vinod Kumar

16. SAB SUKH DATA RAM HAI

Taal: Kaharwa   Chord: CEG   S=D#
Transpose+1 and play from C Scale
https://youtu.be/ztyhlpnRuFU
Bhai Jabartor Singh ji

sab sukh data ram hai,dusar naahin koi

kahu naanak suni re manaa the simrat gati hoy

sukh dukh jeh parse nahin lobh moh abhimaan

kahu naanak suni re manaa so murat bhagwaan

jo sukh ko chaahe sadaa saran ram ki leh

kahu naanak suni re mana durlabh maanakh deh

sukh me bahu sangi bhaye dukh me sang na koy

kahu naanak hari bhaj manaa ant sahaayi hoy

jatan bahut sukh ke kiye dukh ko kiyo na koy

kahu naanak suni re manaa hari bhave so hoy

SAB SUKH DATA RAM HAI

dha	tit	tin	tin	tk	tit	dhin	dhin	dha	tit	tin	tin	tk	tit	dhin	dhin
1	2	3	4	5	6	7	8	1	2	3	4	5	6	7	8
	CD	D	D	D	E	D	C	-	D	E	D	E	-	A	E
	sb	su	kh	da	-	ta	-	-	ra	-	m	hai	-	-	-
-	E	A	G	E	D	E	C	D	-	E	-	D	-	-	-
-	du	s	r	na	-	hi	n	ko	-	-	-	e	-	-	-
-	A	A	-	G	A	E	G	-	G	A	G	A	-	A	E
-	khu	na	-	n	k	su	n	-	re	-	m	na	-	-	-
-	EA	A	G	E	D	E	C	D	-	E	-	D	-	-	-
-	teh	si	m	r	t	g	t	ho	-	-	-	e	-	-	-
-	AA	A	A	G	A	E	G	-	G	A	G	A	-	A	E
-	sukh	du	kh	je	h	p	r	-	se	-	n	hi	-	-	-
-	A	A	G	E	D	E	C	D	-	E	-	D	-	-	-
-	lo	bh	mo	-	h	a	bhi	ma	-	-	-	n	-	-	-
-	AA	A	-	G	A	E	G	-	G	A	G	A	-	A	E
-	khu	na	-	n	k	su	n	-	re	-	m	na	-	-	-
-	EA	A	G	E	D	E	C	D	-	E	-	D	-	-	-
-	so-	mu	-	r	t	bh	g	va	-	-	-	n	-	-	-
-	A	A	A	G	A	E	G	-	G	A	G	A	-	A	E
-	jo	su	kh	ko	-	cha	-	-	he	-	s	da	-	-	-
-	EA	A	G	E	D	E	C	D	-	E	-	D	-	-	-
-	sr	n	ra	-	m	kii	-	le	-	-	-	h	-	-	-
-	A	A	-	G	A	E	G	-	G	A	G	A	-	A	E
-	khu	na	-	n	k	su	n	-	re	-	m	na	-	-	-
-	EA	A	G	E	D	E	C	D	-	E	-	D	-	-	-
-	dur	l	bh	ma	-	n	kh	de	-	-	-	h	-	-	-

Vinod Kumar

17. TU JANAT MAIN KICHHU NAHI

Sabad: Bhagat Ravidas Ji

Singer: Bhai Harjinder Singh Ji

Taal: Kaharwa

Chord: EGB   S=C#

Transpose+1 and play from C Scale

https://youtu.be/hya0lgiDoRc
Bhai Harjinder Singh Ji

tu jaanat main kichhu nahin bhav khandan ram

sagal jeev sarnaagati prabh puran kaam

daaridu dekhi sabh ko hanse aisii dasaa hamaari

ashtdasa sidhi kar tale sabh kripa tumaari

jo teri sarnaagta tin naahi bhaaru

unch neech tumte tare aalaju sansaaru

kahi ravidaas akath katha bahu kaai karijai

jaisa tu taisa tuhi kya upma diijai

TU JANAT MAIN KICHHU NAHI

dha	ge	n	ti	n	ke	dhi	n	dha	ge	n	ti	n	ke	dhi	n
1	2	3	4	5	6	7	8	1	2	3	4	5	6	7	8
	E	-	E	E	F$^\#$	G	-	-	E	F$^\#$	E	D	-	G	G
	tu	-	ja	n	t	mai	-	-	ki	chhu	n	hi	-	bh	v
F$^\#$	-	E	D	E	-	-	-	B	-	G	A	B	-	-	-
khn	-	d	n	ra	-	-	m	music for playing further							-
-	B	B	B	B	D$^{b\prime}$	D'	B	B	D$^{b\prime}$	-	A	A	-	D'	D'
-	sg	l	ji	-	-	-	a	sr	na	-	g	ti	-	pr	bh
D$^{b\prime}$	-	A	A	B	-	-	-								
pu	-	r	n	ka	-	-	m								
-	B	B	B	B	D$^{b\prime}$	D'	B	B	D$^{b\prime}$	-	A	A	-	D'	D'
-	sg	l	ji	-	-	-	a	sr	na	-	g	ti	-	pr	bh
D$^{b\prime}$	-	A	A	B	-	G	F$^\#$	E	E	-	E	E	F$^\#$	G	-
pu	-	r	n	ka	-	-	-	m	tu	-	ja	n	t	mai	-
-	E	F$^\#$	E	D	-	G	G	F$^\#$	-	E	D	E	-	-	-
-	ki	chhu	n	hi	-	bh	v	khn	-	d	n	ra	-	-	m
	B	B	B	B	D$^{b\prime}$	D'	-	B	D$^{b\prime}$	-	B	A	-	-	-
	da	ri	d	de	-	kh	-	sb	ko	-	hn	se	-	-	-
D$^{b\prime}$	-	D$^{b\prime}$		D'	B	D$^{b\prime}$	A	B	-	B					
ae	-	si	-	d	sha	-	h	ma	-	ri	-	-	-	-	-
-	B	B	B	B	D$^{b\prime}$	D'	D'	B	D$^{b\prime}$	D$^{b\prime}$	B	A	-	-	-
-	ash	t	d	sha	-	si	ddh	-	k	r	t	lai	-	-	-
-	-	D'	D'	D$^{b\prime}$	D$^{b\prime}$	-	A	B	-	B	-	-	-	-	-
-	-	s	b	kir	pa	-	tum	ha	-	ri	-	-	-	-	-
-	E	E	E	E	F$^\#$	G	G	-	E	F$^\#$	E	D	-	G	G
-	ash	t	d	sha	-	si	ddh	-	k	r	t	lai	-	s	b

Vinod Kumar

| F♯ | F♯ | - | D | E | - | E | - | - | E | - | E | E | F♯ | G | - |
| kri | pa | - | tum | ha | - | ri | - | - | tu | - | ja | n | t | mai | - |

| - | E | F♯ | E | D | - | G | G | F♯ | - | E | D | E | - | - | - |
| - | ki | chhu | n | hi | - | bh | v | khn | - | d | n | ra | - | - | m |

music: E F♯ G F♯ E F♯ E D, E F♯ G F♯ E - - -
E F♯ G F♯ E F♯ E D, E A G F♯ E - - -
B D♭' D' B D♭' A B, B D♭' D' B D♭' A B-
F♯ E F♯ A G F♯ E , F♯ E F♯ A G F♯ E

| B | - | B | B | D♭' | D' | - | B | D♭' | - | B | A | - | - | - |
| jo | - | te | ri | - | - | - | shr | na | - | g | ta | - | - | - |

| E | F♯ | G | A | B | - | D' | D' | D♭' | - | A | - | B | - | - | - |
| - | - | - | - | - | - | ti | n | na | - | hi | - | bha | - | - | r |

| - | B | B | B | - | D♭' | D' | D' | - | D♭' | - | B | A | - | - | - |
| - | un | ch | ni | - | ch | tu | m | - | te | - | t | re | - | - | - |

| - | - | - | - | - | - | D' | - | D♭' | D♭' | A | - | B | - | - | - |
| - | - | - | - | - | - | aa | - | l | j | sn | - | sa | - | - | r |

| - | E | E | E | - | F♯ | G | - | - | F♯ | - | E | D | - | G | - |
| - | un | ch | ni | - | ch | tu | m | - | te | - | t | re | - | aa | - |

| F♯ | F♯ | D | - | F♯ | - | - | - | - | E | - | E | E | F♯ | G | - |
| l | j | sn | - | sa | - | - | r | - | tu | - | ja | n | t | mai | - |

| - | E | F♯ | E | D | - | G | G | F♯ | - | E | D | E | - | - | - |
| - | ki | chhu | n | hi | - | bh | v | khn | - | d | n | ra | - | - | m |

| B | B | B | B | D♭' | D' | - | B | B | D♭' | B | A | - | - | - |
| kh | r | vi | da | - | s | - | a | k | th | k | tha | - | - | - |

| E | F♯ | G | A | B | - | D' | D' | D♭' | - | A | A | B | - | B | - |
| - | - | - | - | - | - | b | hu | ka | - | e | k | ri | - | jai | - |

| - | B | - | B | B | D♭' | D' | - | B | B | D♭' | B | A | - | - | - |
| - | jai | - | sa | tu | - | - | - | tai | sa | - | tu | hi | - | - | - |

E	F#	G	A	B	-	D'	-	D♭'	D♭'	A	-	B	-	B	-
-	-	-	-	-	-	kya	-	u	p	ma	-	di	-	jai	-
-	E	-	E	E	F#	G	-	E	E	F#	E	D	-	G	-
-	jai	-	sa	tu	-	-	-	tai	sa	-	tu	hi	-	kya	-
F#	F#	D	-	E	-	E	-	-	E	-	E	E	F#	G	-
u	p	ma	-	di	-	jai	-	-	tu	-	ja	n	t	mai	-
-	E	F#	E	D	-	G	G	F#	-	E	D	E	-	-	-
-	ki	chhu	n	hi	-	bh	v	khn	-	d	n	ra	-	-	m

18. TU PRABH DATA, DANMAT PURA

Film: Halla Bol (2008) Singer: Sukhvinder Singh
Lyrics: Sabad Gurubani Chord: FAC'   S=C#
Taal: Bhajani Theka
Transpose+1 and play from C Scale
https://www.youtube.com/watch?v=Ogw9dDVEzlQ
satnaam shri waheguru
tu prabh data, daan mat pura, ham thaare bhikhari jiyo
main kya maangu kichh thir na rahaayi, har deejai naam piyari
jiyo, tu prabh data.....

ghat ghat rav rahya banvaari, jal thal mahi al gupto vare,
guru shabdi dekh nihaari jiio,
tu prabh data.....

marat pyal, aakaash dikhayo, guru satgur kirpa dhaari jiyo
so brahm ajoni hai bhi honi, ghat bhiitar dekh murari jiyo
tu prabh data.....

janm maran ko, eho jag bapdo, in duje bhagat visari jiyo
satguru mile ta gurmat paaiye, saakat baaji haarii jiyo
tu prabh data.....

satguru bandhan tod niraare, bahor naa garbh manjhaari jiyo
naanak gyan ratan pargaasyaa, har man vasya nirankaari jiyo
main kya maangun... tu prabh data... satnaam waaheguru....

Vinod Kumar

TU PRABH DATA, DANMAT PURA

dhin	-	n	dhin	-	dhi	n	n	dhin	-	n	tin	-	ti	n	n
1	2	3	4	5	6	7	8	9	10	11	12	13	14	15	16

```
GF  F    F   GGFF   G A A G F
stnam    sri  vaheguru------------ ,

A    AG  FF    FF  GF    E---D
tu   prbh data, dan  mt     pu--ra,

D   G GAC'      G  AG   EG F
hm  thare----,   bhikhari  jio,

A    AG   A—F-    FF     F   G   FE D
mai  kya  man--gu- kichhu thir  na   rha ii,

D  EGG  A---GAC'  AG A   EGF
hr  di-jai na--- ---m  pya-ri   ji-o

A  AG   AF
tu prbh data...

C'AB       C'----C'  C'C'   BC'   ABBC'C'
ght---      gh------t   rm    rhya  bnva---ri,

BC' AB  BC' C'C'C'   BC'AB   C' C'C'
jl- thl        m -- hial    gupto-    v-rtai,

E    G G  AC'   GAG   EG F
guru  shbdi  dekh  nihari   jio,

A   AG   FF
tu  prbh  data..

BC'A  BBC'C'   C'BC'A     BBC'C'
mrt     pya---l,  aaka-sh  dikha-yo,

B     BBBC'  AAG    AA   F  F
guru  stgur    kirpa    dhari jio,
```

B   C'A   BC'C'   BC'   AB   C'E'D'E'C'
so brmh ajoni hai- bhi- ho-----ni,

BB   BBC'   BAG   GAA   FF
ght bhitr de-kh murari jio,

A   A   AA^{b}AF
mai kya man--gu,..

BC'A BC'C'   C'   BC' AB BC'C'
jnm- mrn   ko, eh jg bapuron,

B   BC'   AAG   GAGA F F
in dujai bhgt visa-ri jio,

BC'AB   C'C'   C'   BC'AB   C'E'D'E'C'
stguru   milai ta gurmt   pa---iye,

BBC' AG   AGA   F F
sakt baji ha-ri jio,

A   A   AA^{b}AF
mai kya man--gu,

BC'AB   C'C'   BC'A BC'C'
stguru   bndhn tod   nirare,

BBB   C' AAG   G AA   FF
bhor   na grbh manjhari jio,

C'AB C'C'   BC'A FAC'C'C'
nank gyan   rtn   prgasya,

B BC'   A AG   G AA   F F
hr mn   vsya   nirnkari jio,

AG   A FF
mai   kya mangu...

FFF   FFF   GGGA   FFDE
stnam stnam   vaheguru vaheguru -2

Vinod Kumar

19. ADDI RAT PAHAR DE TADKE

Taal: Kaharwa
Transpose+1 and play from C Scale
https://youtu.be/geFqGQXBIPo

Singer: Jagjit Singh
Chord: CEA EGB   S=C#

gazal
addi raat pahar de tadke, akkh vich unidaan radke

laahi lasi sekan desi, vekh leya main jugnu phad ke

apna kamra jhadan lagda, dur kite jad kunda khadke

jo gal taitthon kah na hoyi, o mere vi dil vich radke

sikhad dupahari kal ik raahi, dig payaa apni chhaan vich vadke

jaan rahi naa tere vajo, nabz taan challe dil vi dhadke

ADDI RAT PAHAR DE TADKE

dha	ge	n	ti	n	ke	dhi	n	dha	ge	n	ti	n	ke	dhi	n
1	2	3	4	5	6	7	8	1	2	3	4	5	6	7	8

prelude:
A – B – D' ---- A – B – D' ----
FE ED DC C.B .B.A .B.A---

EEF GEF DEC D.B F-E
addi- ra-t phr de- trke

AA AA GBG F-E
akkh vich uninda rrke

interlude:
EF GE FED- ED-
EF GF AFE- FE

AA AB—AF F$^\#$GA F E
lahi lasi ---- sekn desi

AA AA A BBG F E
vekh laiya mai jugnu fr ke

interlude:
FE FE FA BA BA BC'
BA AG GF FE DE- FE

 EEDC CCGF$^\#$ F$^\#$GA FFE
apna- kmra-- jharn lgda

AA AA AGB BG F E
dur kite jd- kunda khrke

interlude:
EF GE FED- ED-
EF GF AFE- FE

A A AB-G F$^\#$G A FE
jo gl taitho-- kh na hoyi

Vinod Kumar

A   AA   AGB   B   GG   F E
o   mere vi--- dil   vich   rrke

interlude:
FE FE FA BA BA BC'
BA AG GF FE DE- FE
E- FE AE E- FE AD
D- ED ED C.B CD DE FE

EED   CCGF# F#F# GA   FE
sikhr   duphri - kal   ik   rahi

AA   AA   AAAGB B   GG   F E
dig   pya   apni---   chhan   vich   vrke

interlude:
FE FE FA BA BA BC'
BA AG GF FE DE- FE

AA   GA   B   F#GA   F E
jan   rhi   na   tere-   vajo

AAA   A   AAGB   B   G   F E
nbj   ta   chlle--   dil   vi   dhrke

20. ANKHIYA NU RAIN DE

Taal: Kaharwa

Transpose+1 and play from C Scale

https://youtu.be/mQ6qZKVGuq0

Singer: Reshma

Chord: DFA   S=C#

ankhiyaan nu rain de ankhiyaan de kol kol

chan pardesiya bol bhanve na bol

vekhan da cha sannu mukh partavin na

nede nede vassin dhola dur dur jaavin na

dur da khyaal chhad bas ankhiyaan de kol kol

chan pardesiya bol bhanve na bol

murali baja ke jiiven, chad gaiyo raag ve

kanvi siva ke jiiven ban gayo jogi ve

dilaan nu na todin jiiven sajna nu na rol

chan pardesiya bol bhanve na bol

banda main shariyaan sach sarkaar diyaan

muddtaan de baad aaiyaan ghadiyaan pyar diiyaan

ik ik feri saari bani anmol ve

chan pardesiya bol bhanve na bol

Vinod Kumar

ANKHIYA NU RAIN DE

dha	ge	n	ti	n	ke	dhi	n	dha	ge	n	ti	n	ke	dhi	n
1	2	3	4	5	6	7	8	1	2	3	4	5	6	7	8

```
CD.B♭       C   DD  E♭D  DGG       G  FDF  FA
ankhiyaan  nu  rain de- ankhiyaan de kol    kol

AB♭  AB♭----AB♭A GFDE♭   FG  FE♭      D   E♭D
chn  pr-----desiya-------   bol bhanve na  bol

CD.B♭        C    DD  E♭D
ankhiyaan  nu  rain de-

DDF  G   A   AB♭A--   AB♭     AB♭---- AB♭ A G F GA GF E♭
vekhn da  cha sannu--- mukh    pr----tavin  na

AB♭    AB♭G   GA♭ GF   FG DE♭  FG  FE♭  DD   D
nede nede-  vssi--      dhola--  dur dur javin na

CD .B♭  CDD  E♭D  DG  GGG      G  FDF  FA
dur  da   khyal chhd bs ankhiyaan de kol    kol

AB♭  AB♭----AB♭A GFDE♭   FG  FE♭      D   E♭D
chn  pr-----desiya-------   bol bhanve na  bol

DDF GA  A  B♭A     AB♭     AB♭---- AB♭ A G F GA GF E♭
murli bja ke jiven, chdh giyo      ragve

AAB♭ G  GG  A♭GF  FGDE♭  FG  FE♭  DD   D
kanvi- siva ke--- jiven-- ,  bn  gyo jogi  ve

CD .B♭  C  DD  E♭D  DGG  G  DF  FA
dila  nu na todi  jiven sjna   nu na- rol

AB♭  AB♭----AB♭A GFDE♭   FG  FE♭      D   E♭D
chn  pr-----desiya-------   bol bhanve na  bol

CD.B♭         C   DD  E♭D
ankhiyaan  nu  rain de-
```

```
DD    F    GA--BᵇA        ABᵇ  ABᵇ---- ABᵇ  G  A F Eᵇ
bnda  mai  sahri-yaan-    sch  sr-----kar        di  yaan-----


AABᵇG    G    AᵇGF  FGEᵇ    FGF    EᵇD-   D D
muddta-  de   ba-d  aaiyaan ghdiyaan pyar diyaan


CD .BᵇC DD   EᵇD  GG    GGDF  FA
ik   ik feri  sari bni    anmol ve-


ABᵇ  ABᵇ----ABᵇA GFDEᵇ    FG  FEᵇ      D   EᵇD
chn  pr-----desiya-------      bol bhanve na  bol


CD.Bᵇ      C  DD  EᵇD
ankhiyaan  nu  rain de-


CD.Bᵇ      C   DD  EᵇD
ankhiyaan  nu  rain de-
```

21. BAN KE BAHAANRA TE JAWANI SADI

Film: Guddi (1971)   Music: Hansraj Bahal
Lyrics: Verma Malik   Singer: Suman Kalyanpur
Taal: Kaharwa   Chord: DFA   S=C#
Transpose+1 and play from C Scale
https://www.youtube.com/watch?v=nGEmdRbxqPg

ban ke bahaaraan te jawani sadi lut gayi
kise di na tutte rabba jiven sadi tut gayi

lai gaye tainnu vairi te kaleja mera dolya
mar jaane lokkan maithon pyar mera kho leya-2
jaalimaan de hatthon meri duniya ae lut gayi
kise di na tutte rabba jiven sadi tut gayi

chaudavin de channa rataan meriyaan haneriyaan
apne begaaneyaan ne ankhiyaan ne feriyaan-2
ankhiyaan to dur hoyon zindagi ae rus gayi
kise di na tutte rabba jiven sadi tut gayi

Vinod Kumar

BAN KE BAHAANRA TE JAWANI SADI

dha	ge	n	ti	n	ke	dhi	n	dha	ge	n	ti	n	ke	dhi	n
1	2	3	4	5	6	7	8	1	2	3	4	5	6	7	8

EF GB BB C'AC' C' D'C'AGB♭ B♭AG EE FAG-FE
bn ke- bha ra---- te jvani-- sadi- lut gyi------

FF G A FEF FF FG FE EE FAG-
kise di na tutte rbba jiven sadi tut gyi--

D' D' B♭D' C'C' C' B♭D'D' D'D' D'C' D'F'E♭'
lai ge tainnu vairi te kleja mera dolya---

D'D' B♭D' C'C' C'C' D'D' D'D' D' C'D'F'E♭'
mr jane lokka maitho pyar mera kho leya --

D'D' B♭D' C' C'C'
pyar mera kho leya

F'F'F' F' E♭'E♭' D'C'E♭' E♭'D'C' B♭ AF GAB♭
jaliman de httho meri- duniya ae lut g-yi

FF G A FEF FF FG FE EE FAG-
kise di na tutte rbba jiven sadi tut gyi--

D'D'B♭ D' C'C' C'C' D'D'D' D'D'-C'D'F'E♭'
chodvin de chnna rata meriyaan hneriyaan----

D'D'B♭ D'C'C'C' C' D'D'D' D' D'-C'D'F'E♭'
apne beganeyaan ne ankhiyaan ne feriyaan—

D'D'B♭ D' C'C'C'
ankhiyaan ne feriyaan

C'F'F' F' E♭'E♭' D'C'E♭' E♭'D'C' B♭ AF GAB♭-
ankhiyaan to dur hoyo- zindgi ae rus g-yi-

22. BHATTHI WALIYE

Lyrics: Shiv Batalvi   Singer: Asa Singh Mastana
Taal: Kaharwa   Chord: DFA FAC'   S=C#
Transpose+1 and play from C Scale
https://www.youtube.com/watch?v=fJd860GU3u8

aa…….. aa ha aa aa

tainnu deyaan hanjuaan da pada, peedaan da paraga bhun de

o bhatthi waliye

o bhatthi waliye chambe diye daaliye -2

peedaan da paraga bhun de, o bhatthi waliye

o bhatthi waliye

ho gayaa k vela mainnu dhal gaiyaan chhaavan ni

veleyaan chon mud aaiyaan majjiyaan te gavaan ni

paya chidiyaan ne cheek chihada

peedaan da paraga bhun de, o bhatthi waliye

o bhatthi waliye

chheti chheti karin main taan-2 jaana badi dur ni

jitthe mere haaniyaan da dur gaya puur ni

os pind da sunindaraan mada

peedaan da paraga bhun de, o bhatthi waliye

o bhatthi waliye

saun gaiyaan havaanvaan ro ro -2 ghar var lapni

taareyaan nu chad gaya mittha mittha taap ni

janj saanvaan di da rus gaya nada -2

peedaan da paraga bhun de, o bhatthi waliye

o bhatthi waliye

Vinod Kumar

meri vaari patteyaan di pand silli ho gayi

nikki jayi kadahi teri kaannu bhilli ho gayi

tere senk nun ki bajya dugaada

peedaan da paraga bhun de, o bhatthi waliye

o bhatthi waliye

BHATTHI WALIYE

dha	ge	n	ti	n	ke	dhi	n	dha	ge	n	ti	n	ke	dhi	n
1	2	3	4	5	6	7	8	1	2	3	4	5	6	7	8

```
A ----- GA- F    D    A    G   F
aa-----------       aa   ha  aa  aa


AA      GA    AAGA  F AGG  FF  G  AGA   GF  FD
tennu  deyaan  hnjuaa  da  pa-da,  pida  da  praga  bhun  de-


 G   GG  F-G- FF
o  bhtthi  va— liye


C’ C’C’  C’D’C’Bᵇ AA    GF  F- FGA
o  bhtthi  valiye-  chmbe  diye  da-liye-  -2


GA   G  FGA  GF    FD
pida  da  praga  bhun  de-


 G   GG  F-G- FF-  G   GG  F-FF
o  bhtthi  va—liye-   o  bhtthi  va-liye


C’  AC’  C’  D’D’  Eᵇ’Eᵇ’----- D’C’
ho  gya  k  vela  mainnu


C’  AC’  C’  D’D’  Eᵇ’Eᵇ’    C’C’  C’C’    BᵇC’BᵇC’    A-
ho  gya  k  vela  mainnu  dhl  gaiyaan  chha-va-    ni-


C’C’C’        C’    D’C’  BᵇBᵇ   A AG   F  FF  EᵇD
beleyaan    chon  mur  aaiyaan  mjjiyaan  te  gava  ni
```

C'C'   C'D'C'   B^b AG FF- GA
paya chidiyaan ne chik chiha-da-

 GA   G FGA GF FD
pida da praga bhun de-

 G GG F-G- FF G GG   F-FF
o bhtthi va—liye- o bhtthi va-liye

C'A   C'C' D'D' D' E^b' ---- F' E^b' F' D' C'
chheti chheti kri   mai tan---------

C'A   C'C' D'D' E^b' E^b' D'E^b' D'C' C'C' C'-
chheti chheti kri   mai tan jana   bdi   dur ni-

C'C'   C'C'   D'- B^{b}B^b B^b AA GF FF E^{b}D
jitthe mere   ha-niyaan da tur gya pur ni

C'C' C'D' C' AAAGF   F-GA
os   pind da sunndra- mada-

GA   G FGA GF FD
pida da praga bhun de-

 G GG F-G FFD G GG F-FF
o bhtthi va—liye- o bhtthi va-liye

 C'   AC'   C'D'D' E^b' E^b'--------- D'C'E^b'C'
saun giiyaan hvava ro ro ---------

C'   AC'   C'D'D' E^b' E^b' --D'F'-D'C' C'C' C'C' C'C' C' A
saun gaiiyaan hvava ro ro----   ghr vr lap ni----

C'   AC'   C'D'D' E^b' E^b'   E^b'E^b' D'C' C'C' C'A
saun gaiiyaan hvava ro ro---- ghr vr lap ni----

C'C'C'   C' C'D' B^{b}B^b AA   GG FF E^{b}FD
tareyaan   nu chdh gya mittha mittha tap ni—

C'C' C'D' C' B♭ AA GF   F-GA
jnj   sanva di da rus gya   la-da- -2

GA   G FGA GF   FD
pida da praga bhun de-

 G GG F-G FFD G GG F-FF
o bhtthi va—liye-   o bhtthi va-liye

AA   C'C' D'D'E♭' E♭' ---- D'E♭'D'-C'
meri vari ptteyaan di--------

C'A C'C' D'D'E♭' E♭' C'C' C'C' C' B♭AF
meri vari ptteyaan di   pnd   silli ho gyi-

C'C'   C' C'D'C' B♭B♭ AA   GG   F F E♭D
mitti di   kdahi te-ri kannu bhilli ho gyi—

C'C'   C'D' C' B♭ AAG   FF-GA
tere   senk nu kii vjya duga-da-

GA   G FGA GF   FD
pida da praga bhun de-

 G GG F-G FFD G GG F-FF
o bhtthi va—liye- o bhtthi va-liye

23. CHADHDE SURAJ DHALDE VEKHE

Taal: Kaharwa   Chord: CE^{b}G   S=C#
Transpose+1 and play from C Scale

dukkhaan mainnu maar mukaya, sukhan da e kal ni maye

te zindadi maitthon nibhdi naahi, ik vaari fir paal ni maaye

chadhde suraj dhalde vekhe, bujjhe deeve balde vekhe

heere da koi mul na taare, khote sikke chalde vekhe

odi rahmat de naal bande, paani utte chalde vekhe

jinhaan da na jag te koi, o puttar vi palde vekhe

jinhaan kadar na kiti yar di, hath khaali o malde vekhe

loki kainde daal nai galdi, main te patthar galde vekhe

kai pairaan to nange firde, sir te labde chhaanvaan

mainu data sab kuchh ditta, kyon na shukar manaavaan

Vinod Kumar

CHADHDE SURAJ DHALDE VEKHE

dha	ge	n	ti	n	ke	dhi	n	dha	ge	n	ti	n	ke	dhi	n
1	2	3	4	5	6	7	8	1	2	3	4	5	6	7	8

E^bE^b –FD E^bE^b –CDD---C—DD-C--   .A^b.B^b .B^bCC
dukkhan   mainu -------------------   mar   mukaya

CC.B^bF   F DC.B^b DE^bF E^b DC
sukkhan   da e   kal   ni mae

F FFG   G$B^b$$A^b$$B^b$ GF GA^{b}D'D' D'–-C'D'F'E^b'F'----DC'
te jinddi   mai-----tho   nibh-di   na-------------- hi

D'D'   C' $B^b$$A^b$ GA^{b}D' C' C'C'
sukkhan   da e --   kal   ni   mae

GGD' C'$B^b$$A^b$ G F DE^bG F E^bDC-D-C-.B^b D F F D-C
ik   vari   fir   pal   ni ma-e----------   pa l   ni ma-e

music: G B^b C' D' C' , E^b'---C' D'---C' B^b C' E^b' D' C' -x2

.B^bCDC   .B^b.G.G .B^bDDC DFE^bF DC
chdhde   surj   dhlde   ve-----khe----

GGF   G$B^b$$A^b$$B^b$ GFE^b E^bGG F–DC
bujjhe di-------ve--   blde   ve—khe---

C'C'   BC'   A^{b}G   GA^b C' A^{b}G
hire   da-   koi   mul na   tare

C'C'   C'B^bD'C'   A^{b}G   GA^b C' FE^bDC
hire   da------   koi   mul na   ta---re

.B^bCDC   .B^b.G.G   .B^bDDC DFE^bF DC
khote   sikke   chlde   ve-----khe--

music: flute: E^b' ----C' D' – C' B^b C' D' C'

$E^b$$E^b$D $E^b$$E^bDE^b$ .G .B^b.B^b CC
odi   rhmt   de nal   bnde

E^{b}E^{b}D E^{b}E^{b}GG   D FE^b DCDF
odi   rhmt   de nal bnde---

E^{b}E^{b}D E^{b}E^{b}DE^b .G .B^b.B^b CC
odi   rhmt   de nal   bnde

C'C'   E^b'D'C'B^b G B^{b}A^b GB^{b}A^{b}C'
odi   rhmt   de nal bn-de-

C'C'   B^{b}C'A^{b}B^{b}G G C'B^b GFDC
odi   rhmt   de nal   bnde----

.B^{b}CDC   .B^b.G   .B^{b}DDC   DFE^{b}F DC
 pa-ni-   utte   chlde   ve----khe--

C'C'B^b C' A^{b}G GA^b C'B^b A^{b}GA^{b}C'
jinha da na- jg te- koii

C'C'B^b C' A^{b}G GA^b C'B^b A^{b}G
jinha da na- jg te- koii

E^b'E^b'D'   E^b' D'C'B^b A^{b}A^b B^b C'—B^{b}A^b GA^{b}C'
jinha   da na--- jg   te ko—ii— ii---

C'C'B^b B^{b}E^b'D'C'   A^{b}G GA^b C' GFDC
jinha   da-----   na- jg te ko---ii

.B^{b}C DC.B^b.B^b .G .B^{b}DDC DFE^{b}F DC
o-   pu-ttr   vi plde--   ve-----khe—

.B^{b}CDC .B^b.G.G .B^{b}DDC DFE^{b}F DC
chdhde surj   dhlde   ve----- khe—

music: flute: E^b' ----C' D' – C' B^b C' D' C'

C' C' D' C' B^b A^b G F G A^b B^b A^b C'
buleya.......

Vinod Kumar

G G B♭ B♭ C' C' D' ----C' D' C' B♭ A♭ B♭ G
buleya.......

C'C'C'B♭F'E♭' E♭'E♭' D'D'D' C' C'D'B♭ B♭D'D' D'
buleya   jinha kdr   na kiiti   yar   di

C'C'D' – C'A♭B♭A♭B♭A♭B♭C'
buleya..........................

 D'D' C'D'D' C' B♭C'B♭G GA♭C' B♭ A♭GGB♭A♭C'
jinha kdr   na kii-ti-   ya-r   di, buleya

C'C' B♭D'C' B♭ A♭B♭A♭G GA♭C' B♭ GFDC
jinha kdr   na kii-ti-   ya-r   di, buleya

.B♭C DC.B♭ .G .B♭DDC   DFE♭F DC
hth   kha-li   o mlde-   ve------khe-- -2

GG FGGB♭A♭B♭ GFE♭-G GG GF GC'B♭ A♭GFE♭
hth kha----li-   o-   hth kha-li---- o-
E♭A♭GF F– DC
mlde   ve-khe

lokii kainde dal ni gldi, mai te ptthr glde vekhe
kii paira to nnge firde, sir te lbhde chhava
mainu data sb kuchh ditta, kyon na shukr mnava

24.   CHANN KITHAN GUZARI AAI RAT

Punjabi Lok Geet
Taal: Kaharwa
Transpose+1 and play from C Scale
https://youtu.be/x0Va68pBXO0

Singer: Surinder Kaur
Chord: CE^{b}G   S=C#

chann kitthan guzari aayi

o chann kitthan guzari aayi raat ve

mainda ji dalilaan de vaat ve

o chann kitthan guzari aayi

kothe te fir kothada mahi kothe sukda gha bhalaa

aashiqaan jodiyaan paudiyaan te maashukaan jode rah bhalaa

o chann kitthan guzari aayi

kothe te fir kothada mahi kothe sukdi ret bhalaa

asaan gundhaaiyaan meendiyaan tu kise bahaane vekh zara

o chann kitthan guzari aayi

kothe te fir kothda maahi kothe te tandur bhalaa

pahli roti tu khavein to tende saathi nasde dur bhalaa

o chann kitthan guzari aayi

Vinod Kumar

CHANN KITHAN GUZARI AAI RAT

dha	ge	n	ti	n	ke	dhi	n	dha	ge	n	ti	n	ke	dhi	n
1	2	3	4	5	6	7	8	1	2	3	4	5	6	7	8

prelude and interlude:
(CDDC DE^{b}E^{b}D E^{b}FFE^b E^{b}DDC
CDDC DE^{b}E^{b}D CD-- E^{b}D--) x2

(B^b B^{b}A AG GF
A AG GF FE^b
G GF FE^b E^{b}D
B^{b}AG E^{b}FD) x2

C.B   CCD D D D   D (AGFE^{b}D)
chnn   kitha- gujari   aaii

 C C.B   CCD   D D D   D   FE F
 o   chnn   kitha- gujari aaii   rat ve

DE^{b}C   DF FFGGA F   FE^{b}E^b E^b
maidan- ji-   dli-la-   de va-t   ve

 D C.B   CCD   D D D   D (AGFE^{b}D)
 o   chnn   kitha- gujari   aaii

DE^b F   G   GGG   AA   FF E^{b}E^{b}F   E^b E^{b}FD
kothe te fir kothda manhi kothe sukda gha bhla-

 DDE^b FGG   GGG   A   GFF   E^{b}F   E^b E^{b}F
aashika jodiyaan paudiyaan te mashukan jode rah bhla

 D C.B   CCD   D D D D (AGFE^{b}D)
 o   chnn   kitha- gujari aaii

DE^b F   G   GGG   AA   FF E^{b}E^{b}F   E^b E^{b}FD
kothe te fir kothda manhi kothe sukdi ret bhla-

 DD   E^{b}F G   GGG   A FF FE^{b}F   E^b E^{b}F
asan gundhaiiyaan mindiyaan tu kise bhane vekh zra

```
D  C.B   CCD   D D D   D   (AGFEbD)
o  chnn   kitha- gujari  aaii

DEb    F   G   GGG   AA   FF   Eb   FEb    EbFD
kothe te  fir  kothda manhi kothe te  tandur bhla-

 D Eb   FG  G   GG    G  AA    FF    EbF   Eb   EbF
phli     roti tu khaven o tainde sathi  nsde dur bhla

D  C.B   CCD   D D D   D   (AGFEbD)
o  chnn   kitha- gujari   aaii
```

25. HAY O RABBA NAIYON LAGDA

Taal: Kaharwa   Singer: Reshma
Transpose+1 and play from C Scale   Chord: DF#A   S=C#
https://youtu.be/d5b0Gob0HIE

shahar bhambar di kudiyon tusi nak vich nath na paayo
main bhul gaiyaan tusi bhul na jaaiyo yaar naal baloch na layo

haay o rabba naiyo lagda dil mera
o ho ho ho rabba naiyo lagda dil mera
naiyo lagda dil mera
haay o rabba naiyo lagda dil mera

sajna baje hoya hanera
haay o rabba naiyo lagda dil mera
jogi baitha been bajaave dil mere nu chain n aave
nas pai sapni roye sapera
haay o rabba naiyo lagda dil mera

sasari tun ba mataa devein
tu na ja, bilocha yaari
agli raat kya majnaan di

Vinod Kumar

te pichhli raat taiyaari
kothed chadh ke main jhaatiyaan maaraan
lag uth vaindi kataari
dar di maari haank na maaraan
main te shaq pai jaave yaari

dasso ni ilaaj koi tutte hoye dil da
karun ki bahaana dilbar nahin milda
chaar chhafere hoya hanera
haay o rabba naiyo lagda dil mera

(In this song Sa is taken as C# as most of the people use this Sa.)
(Reshma ji's Sa was .A#)

HAY O RABBA NAIYON LAGDA

dhage nti nkedhin	dhage nti nke dhin	dhage nti nkedhin	dhage nti nkedhin
12 34 56 78	12 34 56 78	12 34 56 78	12 34 56 78

prelude: D' C' B♭ A G F# A--

AB♭   AAB♭   A AAAF# AA AA AA AA B♭ AA-AF#
shahr bhambar di kudiyo   tusi nk vich nth na payo

B♭A GF# EDD DD DD ED B♭ B♭ A
mai- bhul giyaan tusi bhul na jayo

.G.B♭ .A.A .B♭DC .B♭ .A.A
yar nal bloch na layo

music: A B♭ AB♭ AG A B♭ A -2

.A .A .B♭C ED C.B♭.AC .B♭.A .A.A
hay o rbba niyo lgda-- dil mera

.A .A .B♭C .B♭C .B♭.A.A D E D.B♭
hay o rbba niyo lgda dil mera

.A.B^b .A.A.A .B^b .A.A
niyo   lgda   dil mera

.A .A .B^{b}C .B^{b}C   .B^b.A.A .B^b.A .A.A
hay o rbba niyo   lgda   dil   mera

DDD   DCF$^#$F$^#$ EF$^#$E   DDD-C.B^{b}C.A
sjna   ba---j   ho-ya   hnera ---------

.A .A .B^{b}C .B^{b}C .B^b.A.A D E D.B^b
hay o rbba niyo lgda   dil mera

.A.B^b .A.A.A .B^b .A.A
niyo   lgda   dil mera

 D   F$^#$ A----- B^{b}AB^{b}AF$^#$
o   ho ho----- ho

B^{b}A   AA   B^{b}AA B^{b}A AF$^#$D
rbba niyo lgda   dil   mera-

EEG EDC.B^b C.B^b .A.A
niyo   lgda-   dil mera

.A   .A .B^{b}C ED   C.A.A-C .B^b.A .A.A
hay o rbba niyo   lgda--   dil   mera -2

F$^#$GB^b A-GAF$^#$ F$^#$G B^{b}A-^{G}A B^{b}A F$^#$E F$^#$D CD   E   DD
jogi   bai-tha-- bin bja-ve- dil mere nu- chain n aave

F$^#$F$^#$ GB^b AA-GAF$^#$ AG F$^#$ED-CDC.B^b.A
ns   paii sp-ni--   roye snpera-----------

.A   .A .B^{b}C ED   C.B^b.AC .B^b.A .A.A
hay o rbba niyo   lgda-   dil   mera

DDD   DCF$^#$F$^#$ EF$^#$E DDD-C.B^{b}C.A
sjna   ba---j   ho-ya   hnera ---------

Vinod Kumar

```
.A    .A .BᵇC  ED    C.Bᵇ.AC  .Bᵇ.A  .A.A
hay  o  rbba niyo  lgda-      dil   mera -2


.A    .A  .BᵇC .BᵇC .Bᵇ.A.A  D E  D.Bᵇ
hay  o  rbba niyo  lgda      dil  mera

.A.Bᵇ  .A.A.A .Bᵇ  .A.A
niyo  lgda    dil  mera

AAA   A  Bᵇ  AA   F#ED
ssri  tu  ba  mta deven

A   A   A-F#  AABᵇA  AAF#
tu  na  ja-,   bilocha yari

AABᵇA  F#E  DD    DDD   ED.Bᵇ
agli-   rat  kya   mjna  di

.G .G.Bᵇ.A  ᴰED.Bᵇ  .A.A.A
te pichhli  ra-t       taiyari

ABᵇA   AA    Bᵇ  A  AAA    GAAF#
kother chdh   ke mai jhatiyaan ma-ra-

AA  AA  ABᵇA  AAAF#
lg   uth vendi- katari-

AA  BᵇA  F#ED  DD   D  DED.Bᵇ
dr  di-  mari-  haak na mara---

.G .Bᵇ .A.A .A  EDED.Bᵇ  .A.A
m te  shk pai ja----ve  yari

AA    Bᵇ AAA  AA-F#  F#F#   BᵇA AA  F#E-GABᵇ-
dsso ni ilaj    koii--    tute  hoe dil  da------

GBᵇ   A AAA  AA-F#  F#F#   AA  BᵇBᵇ Bᵇ
dsso ni ilaj   koii-   tute   hoe dil da
```

AB♭ A   F#EF#D DDCC DE   DDD
krun kii bhana-   dilbr   niyo   milda

F#G B♭AGF# GF#E DDC-.B♭C.A
char chhfere hoya hnera-------

.A   .A .B♭C ED   C.B♭.AC .B♭.A .A.A
hay o rbba niyo lgda--   dil   mera -2

DDD   DCF#F#   EF#E DDD-C.B♭C.A
sjna   ba---j   ho-ya hnera ---------

.A   .A .B♭C ED   C.B♭.AC .B♭.A .A.A
hay o rbba niyo lgda--   dil   mera

.A   .A .B♭C .B♭C .B♭.A.A D E D.B♭
hay o rbba niyo lgda   dil   mera

.A.B♭ .A.A.A .B♭ .A.A
niyo   lgda   dil mera

D   F#   A   B♭AB♭AF#
o   ho ho ho

B♭A   AA   B♭AA B♭A AF#ED
rbba niyo lgda   dil   mera-

EEG EDC.B♭ C.B♭ .A.A
niyo   lgda-   dil mera

.A   .A .B♭C ED   C.B♭.AC .B♭.A .A.A
hay o rbba niyo lgda--   dil   mera -2

Vinod Kumar

26. HEER

Film: Mera Naam Joker (1970)   Music: Jaikishan
Lyrics: Prem Dhawan   Singer: Md. Rafi
Taal: -   Chord: CE^bG, CE^bA S= F
Transpose+5 and play from C Scale
https://youtu.be/iElpMlllf54

sadke heer tujh pe ham fakir sadke,
tujh se lut kar tere hi dwar aaye
tu to fulon ki sej pe ja baithi,
mere hisse me rahon ke khar aaye

jhuthe vaade the tere vafa jhuthi
khote saude me zindagi haar aaye
yahi ishq hai to kah do duniya se
kisi but pe na kisi ko pyar aaye

de de dil hamara hame wapas
jogi le kar yahi pukar aaye
aur mange jo kuchh to maut mange
tere dar pe hai aakhri bar aaye
jogi le kar yahi pukar aaye

HEER

dha	ge	n	ti	n	ke	dhi	n	dha	ge	n	ti	n	ke	dhi	n
1	2	3	4	5	6	7	8	1	2	3	4	5	6	7	8

CC   CDD D   D C   CCD   DDD- F- E^bDC-
sdke   hir   tujh pe hm   fkiir   sdke

C   C CD D   DE^bD D DF   D FGB^b AB^bG
tujh se lut kr   tere- hi dwar aaye--------

G G GA   G   GF   E^b FE^{b}G   E^{b}D - B^{b}AGFD
tu to fulo   kii sej pe ja--   baithi

CC   CCD   D   DD   E^{b}DC C.A.AF   E^{b}D
mere   hisse- me raho ke--   kha-----r   aaye

AA   AA A AB^{b}A   AAC' B^{b}A- B^{b}AGFDC
jhuthe vade the tere-   vfa-   jhuthi

CC   CD   D DDE^{b}DD   F   FE^b FGB^b- A- B^{b}G
khote saude me zindgi   har   aaye

GG GAG F   G   FG   FE^{b}G   E^{b}GFE^b D- B^{b}AGFD
yhi ishq hai- to kh-   do--   duni-ya se

CC CD D D DD   E^{b}D C.A.AF E^{b}D
kisi but pe n kisi   ko- pya----r aaye

D' D' D'   D'D'D'   D'D'C'E$^{b'}$ D'D'D'   GB^{b}D'
de-de dil   hmara   hme--   vaps   (chord)

 D'D'   D'C'E$^{b'}$ D'C' B^{b}A AGB^b AA   E^{b}GB^b
jogi   le--   kr   yhi   pukar aaye (chord)

B^b B^{b}B^b A B^{b}B^b B^b AC'B^b AG- GD'C'B^{b}GFDC
aur mange jo kuchh to mau-t   mange

CC   CD D D DDE^b C.A.AF E^{b}D
tere   dr pe hai aa-khiri-   ba----r   aaye

CC CD DD DE^{b}D DDB^b- AGFE^{b}DF   E^{b}D
jogi le- kr yhi- puka---------r   aaye.

Vinod Kumar

27. IK MERI ANKH KASHNI

Lyrics: Shiv Kumar Batalvi   Singer: Surinder Kaur
Taal: Kaharwa   Chord: CEG GD   S=C#
Transpose+1 and play from C Scale
https://youtu.be/fBUQWej9F0w

ni ik meri ankh kaashni duja raat de unindare ne maareya
shiishe nu tared pai gayi baal vondi ne dhyan jadon maareya
ni ik meri ankh kaashni duja raat de unindare ne maareya

ik meri sass nivari bhaidi raahi de kikkar ton kaali
galle katthe veer bhundi nit deve mere ma peyaan nu gaali
ni kehda us chandri da ni main laachiyaan da baag ujaadya
ni ik meri ankh kaashni duja raat de unindare ne maareya

duja mera deyor nikda, bhaida goriyaan ranna da shauki
dhuk dhuk nehde baithda, rakh saamne rangiili chaunki
ni isse gal ton dardi, aje teek vi na ghund nu utaareya
ni ik meri ankh kaashni duja raat de unindare ne maareya

teeja mera kant jinven raat channi ch dudh da katora
fikke sinduri rang da, ode naina ch gulabi dora
ni ikko gal maadi usdi, laailag nu hai maa ne vigaadeya

IK MERI ANKH KASHNI

dha	ge	n	ti	n	ke	dhi	n	dha	ge	n	ti	n	ke	dhi	n
1	2	3	4	5	6	7	8	1	2	3	4	5	6	7	8
prelude:															
DD^b- DED^{b}D- 4															
D'- D^b'D^b'D'—															
D'D' C'C' AA GG															
D^b- DE D^{b}D-															

```
G  GE   ED   DbD   DDD
ni ik    meri ankh kashni


DD  CC  E  EEED    Db  DEE
duja rat  de unnindre  ne mareaa


EG      E  DDbD  D  DD
shiishe te tred   pai gyi


DD   CE    E  EEG  EDb   DEE
bal vaundii  ne dhyan jdon mareaa


G  GE   ED   DbD   DDD
ni ik    meri ankh kashni


DD  CC  E  EEED    Db  DEE
duja rat  de unindre  ne mareaa


G  GE   ED   DbD   DDD
ni ik    meri ankh kashni


music:
DDb- DE  DbD-2
D Db D E G A--


EE  GG  AA   AAA
ik    meri sass nivri


AA     AA  A  AGA   BA  F#G
bhaidi rahi de kikr    to- kali


EE  GG    A  AAA
glle-kaththe vir bhunndi
```

```
AA  GA  AA    G AB      A F#G-E
nale deve mere man-pyaan nu gali

E GG    ED  DᵇDD        D
ni kehda us  chndri (buri) da -2

D  D    CCE    E ED  Dᵇ DEE
ni  mai lachiyaan da bag ujadaa

G  GE  ED   DᵇD  DDD
ni ik     meri ankh kashni

DD  CC  E  EEED    Dᵇ DEE
duja rat  de unindre ne mareaa

G  GE  ED   DᵇD  DDD
ni ik     meri ankh kashni
```

28. KALI TERI GUT TE PARANDA

Taal: Kaharwa

Transpose+1 and play from C Scale

Singer: Asa Singh Mastana

Chord: FAC' GBᵇD'   S=C#

https://youtu.be/liq3x6G__2w

kaali teri gut te paraanda tera laal ni
ruup di ae raaniye paraande nu sambhaal ni

ho, kanna vich bunde tere rup da shingar ni
mitthe tere bol muhon bol ik vaar ni
pairaan pondiye nii teri moraan jayi chaal ni
kaali teri gut te paraanda tera laal ni

ho, chand jahe mukhde te gith gith laaliyaan
mahak di jawani jinven chambe diiyaan daaliyaan
jhalli naiyon jaandi tere rup vaali chaal ni
kaali teri gut te paraanda tera laal ni

ho, dheeye ni panjab diye giddeyaan di raani tun
khetaan di bahaar a te chaunke di savaali tun
pyar di pujaarne payaraan da sawaal ni
kaali teri gut te paraanda tera laal ni

KALI TERI GUT TE PARANDA

dha	ge	n	ti	n	ke	dhi	n	dha	ge	n	ti	n	ke	dhi	n
1	2	3	4	5	6	7	8	1	2	3	4	5	6	7	8

prelude:
G--A GF GF B$^\flat$A B$^\flat$A GF GF C'B$^\flat$ C'B$^\flat$ AG B$^\flat$A G- x2

FB$^\flat$ B$^\flat$A AG G AGF   FG G- G   GF FG G- G-
kali teri gut te paranda tera lal ni music:

GC' C' C' C'AA D'C'C'   A GG- F
rup di ae raniye parande   nu snbhal ni

interlude:
G--A GF GF B$^\flat$A B$^\flat$A GF GF C'B$^\flat$ C'B$^\flat$ AG B$^\flat$A G- x2

D'----------- C'F'E'D' D'-----------
ho...

C'C' C'D' D'D' D'D' C'C' C' D'D'- D'
kanna vich bunde tere rup da shingar ni

C'F' F'E' E'D' D'D'   C' C'D' D'- D'
mitthe tere bol munhon bol ik var ni

C'C' C'C'C' A AD' C'C' AA G F
paila paundie ni teri mora jehi chal ni

FB$^\flat$ B$^\flat$A AG G AGF FG G- G GF FG G- G-
kali teri gut te prada tera lal ni music:

interlude:
G--A GF GF B♭A B♭A GF GF C'B♭ C'B♭ AG B♭A G- x2

D'----------- C'F'E'D' D'-----------
ho...

C'C'   C'D'   D'D'D'   D' C'C'   C'D'   D'D'D'
chnn   jhe   mukhde te gith   gith   laliyaan

C'   F'   E'E'D'   D'D'   C'C'   C'D'   D'D'D'
mhk di   jvani   jiven chmbe diyaan daliyaan

C'C' C'C' C'A AD' C'C' AA   G   F
jhlli   niiyo jandi tere rup vali chal ni

FB♭   B♭A AG G AGF FG G-   G   GF FG G- G-
kali   teri gut te prada tera lal ni   music:

interlude:
G--A GF GF B♭A B♭A GF GF C'B♭ C'B♭ AG B♭A G- x2

D'----------- C'F'E'D' D'-----------
ho...

C'C'   C' D'D' D'D' C'C'C'   D' D'D'   D'
dhiye   ni pnjab diye giddeyaan di rani tu

C'F'   F'   E'E'D'   D' D' C'C'   C' D'D'D'   D'
kheta di   bhar   a te chonke di svali   tu

C'   C'   C'C'A   D'C'C' A AG- F
pyar di pujarne pyara da sval ni

FB♭   B♭A AG G AGF   FG G-   G   GF FG G- G-
kali   teri gut te paranda tera lal ni   music:

29. KAKA JAMM PEYA

Lok Geet   Singer: Asa Singh Mastana
Taal: Kaharwa   Chord: GBD'   S=C#
Transpose+1 and play from C Scale
https://youtu.be/8Th2yTxtj4k
mainnu lokkaan ditti vadhayi kaka jam peya

ghar vaali aakhdi patase te manga deyo
main aakhaan gali vich mungfali varta deyo
saadi laggi hon ladaayi kaka jam peya

yaar mangan feestaan te luttan lokon pai gaiyaan
ik do rupaiye de ke suut bahana lai gaiyaan
gal sabnaa khaldi laayi kaka jam peya

note gharon muk gaye te bhattha sada bai gaya
tera sau rupaiye vich kaka sanu pai gaya
badi mahngi payi vadhaayi kaka jam peya

KAKA JAMM PAIYA

dha	ge	n	ti	n	ke	dhi	n	dha	ge	n	ti	n	ke	dhi	n
1	2	3	4	5	6	7	8	1	2	3	4	5	6	7	8

prelude aur interlude:
D' C' B AB B A G D' C' B AB B A G
C' D' C' D' –A AB AB G F#G GA- AA F#G F#AG
C' D' C' D' –A AB AB G F#G GA- AA F#G F#AG

GA   AB   AA   AF#F#   GA   G   GG
mainnu lokan ditti   vdhaii   kaka   jmm   paiya

music: for repeating F#G F#A G- A- F#G F#A G- 2
interlude: D' C' B AB B A G D' C' B AB B A G
C' D' C' D' –A AB AB G F#G GA- AA F#G F#AG -2

Vinod Kumar

D'   C'B D'D'D'   D'D'E' D' C'A   BBG
ghr vali aakhdi   ptase   te manga deyo-

B   AG   GG AA   BBBA AG   GG
mai aakhan gli   vich   mungfli vrta   deyo

GA   AB   AA   AF#F# GA   G   GG
sadi lggi hon   ldaii   kaka jmm paiya

mainnu lokan ditti..

D'   C'B   D'D'D'   D' D'E' D'C' A BBG
yar mangn feestan te luttan loko pai giiyaan

BB A GGG   A A BB   AA G   GG
ik   do rupaiye de ke sut   bhaina lai giiyaan

GA   ABB AAA   F#F#   GA   G   GG
gl   sbna khldi   laii   kaka jmm paiya

mainnu lokan ditti..

D'D'   C'B   D'D' D'D' D' D'E'   D'C' A   BBG
not   ghro muk gye   te bhttha sada bai gya-

AB   A   GGG   AA   AB   AA   G   GG
tera sau rupaiye vich kaka sanu pai gya

GA   AB   AA   AF#F# GA   G   GG
bdi mehngi paii   vdhaii kaka jmm paiya

mainnu lokan ditti..

30. KALE RANG DA PARANDA

Lok Geet   Taal: Kaharwa   Singer: Surinder Kaur, Narinder Kaur
Transpose+1 and play from C Scale   Chord: CEG   S=D

https://youtu.be/gTW2xyoKq_I

kale rang da paraanda mere sajna ne aanda

ni main chum chum ni main chum chum rakhdi firaan

te pabba bhar nachdi firaan

kala ae paraanda naal mehndiyaan vi kaaliyaan

ambri ghataawaan aaj kaaliyaan -2

khushi vich nachchaan mere naal paiyaan nachdiyaan

kannaan vich paiyaan hoiyaan vaaliyaan -2

ni main kuj kuj-2 jhakdi firaan,

te pabba bhar nachdi firaan

sajna da hasa mainnu de gaya dilasa

ode kadmaan ch rakh deyaan dil ni -2

fullan utte jivein koi bhaunr baitha gaanwda

inj ode mukhde da til ni

haay inj ode mukhde da til ni

ni main luk luk-2 takdi firaan,

te pabba bhar nachdi firaan

rud pud jana chann ambraan da adiyo ni

mainnu fir luk luk takda ae -2

ambraan te rab di hawa sathi chaldi ni

taaiyon onu chakna ne dakda ae-2

ni main ankhiyaan nu dakdi firaan,

te pabba bhar nachdi firaan

Vinod Kumar

KALE RANG DA PARANDA

dha	ge	n	ti	n	ke	dhi	n	dha	ge	n	ti	n	ke	dhi	n
1	2	3	4	5	6	7	8	1	2	3	4	5	6	7	8

music: D D E D E- C C E C D-

DC   CD D   EED   DC   CDD   E   ED
kale rng da paranda   mere   sjna   ne aanda

D C   CD   DE   E D   CD   DE EDD   DD C
ni mai chum chum, ni mai chum chum rkhdi   firan

C CD   E   EDD   D D
te pbba bhr nchdi fira

music: D D E D E- C C E C D-

 DD D AAA   AA G G G   G G G
kala e paranda nal mehndiyaan vi kaliyaan

 FFF   FED   DC CD DDE
ambri   ghtava aaj   ka-liyaan-

 GFF   FED   DC CD D D -
ambri ghtava   aaj   ka-liyaan

 DD   DA AA   AA   G   GG   GGGG
khushii vich nchcha mere nal piyaan nchdiyaan

 FF FE   ED   D C   CD DD E
knna vich paiyaan hoiyaan va-liyaan-

 GF FE   ED   D C   CD D D-
knna vich piyaan hoiyaan va-liyaan-

D C   CD DE   EDD   DD C
ni mai kuj kuj -2 jhkdi   fira

C CD   EE   EDD   D D
te pbba bhr   nchdi fira

kale rng da paranda----

music: D D E D E- C C E C D-

DDD   A AA   AA   G GG GGG   GG
sjna   da hasa mainnu de gya dilasa ode

FFF   E ED DC   CD DE
kdman ch rkh deyaan dil   ni-

DE   GFF   E ED   DC   CD   D-
ode   kdman ch rkh deyaan dil   ni

D D DA AA AA   D   DG   GGG
fullan utte jiven koii bhonr baitha gavda

FF   FE EDD   C CD   DE
inj   ode mukhde da til   ni-

E   GF FE EDD   C CD   D
hay inj   ode mukhde da til   ni

D C   CD DE   EED   D D C
ni mai luk   luk-2   tkdi   fira

C CD   E EDD   D D
te pbba bhr nchdi fira

kale rng da paranda----

music: D D E D E- C C E C D--

DD   DA AA AA   GGG   G GGG   G
rur   pur jana chnn ambra da adiyo ni

FF   FE ED   DC CDD   D E- G
mainnu fir   luk   luk tkda   e

GF   FE   ED DC CDD   D -
mainnu fir   luk   luk tkda   e

```
DDD     A AA A  AG  GG   GGG    G
ambra   te rb di hva sathi chldi   ni


 GF   FE   EDD   C  CDD   D E
taiyo onu   chkna nu dkda  e-


GF   FE    EDD  C CDD   D
taiyo onu   chkna ne dkda  e


D  C    CDD    E EDD   D D C
ni mai ankhiyaan nu dkdi    fira-


C  CD   E  EDD   D D
te pbba bhr nchdi   fira
```

31. KI PUCHHDE HO HAAL

Gazal

Lyrics: Shiv Kumar Batalvi

Taal: Kaharwa

Transpose+1 and play from C Scale

https://youtu.be/p9vJuy77TKU

Singer: Gulam Ali

Chord: CE^bG S=C#

ki puchhde ho hal fakiiran da, sada nadiyon vichhde niiraan da

sada hanj di june aaiyaan da sada dil jalyaan dilgeeraan da

eh jaandeyaan kuj shokh jahe rangaan da na tasveeraan hai

jad hatti gaye asi ishqe di, mul kar baithe tasveeraan da

sannu lakkhaan da tan lab gaya, par ik da man vi na miliya

kya likheya kise muqaddar si hatthaan deeyaan chaar lakeeran da

taqdeer ta apni saukan si, tadbeeraan sathon na hoiyaan

naa jang chhuteya na kan pate jhund langh gaya inj heeran da

mere geet vi lok suneende ne nale kafir aakh sadeende ne

main dard nu kaba kah baitha, rab naan rakh baitha peedaan da main daanashwaraan suneendiyaan sang kai vari uchchi bol peya

kujh maan si sahnu ishqe da kujh dava vi si peedaan da

tu khud nu aakal kahnda hain, main khud nu ashiq dasdaa haan

eh lokaan te chhad daiye, kihnu maan ne dende peeraan da

KI PUCHHDE HO HAAL

dha	ge	n	ti	n	ke	dhi	n	dha	ge	n	ti	n	ke	dhi	n
1	2	3	4	5	6	7	8	1	2	3	4	5	6	7	8

prelude:
DCD .A C D - - D - - D – D - - - -
DCD .A C E^b - - E^b - - E^b – E^b - - - -
DE^{b}GAC' A – A G – G
   AC' A – A G – G
   AC' C' – C' A – A G – G E^b – E^b D –
   DD E^{b}D x4

C.AD DDD D DD E^{b}G-AG E^{b}DE^{b}C
kii-- puchhde ho hal fkiira da-----,

DE^b GGG GGG C'AG E^{b}D
sada ndiyo vichhde nira da

C.AD DD D DD E^{b}G-AG E^{b}DE^{b}C
sada hnjh di june aaiyaan da----,

DE^b GG GGG GGC'AG E^{b}D
sada dil jlyaan dilgira da

C.A DDD D DE^b GAGE^{b}D D
kii-- puchhde ho hal fkiira da-

Vinod Kumar

interlude:
E♭ G A - - - - - C' – A G - - - -
E♭ F F E♭ - - - - G – F# – F# F – F E♭ – D –
E♭ G A –

A   AAAA   AA AC'D' C'AG
eh jandeyaan kuj shokh jahe

C'C'   C' D'C' AGC'E♭' D'-C'A
rnga   da na-   tsvira   hai---,

GGAGE♭D D
tsvira   hai

C.A   DD DD DD   E♭GAG E♭DE♭C
jd   htti gaye asi   ishke di----,

DE♭ GG GG   GGC'AG E♭D
mul   kr   baithe tsvira   da

AA   AA   A AA C'D' C'AG
sannu lkkhan da tn   lb   gya-,

C'C' C'C' C' C'D' AG C'   E♭'D'D'
pr   ik   da mn vi   na   miliya

C.AD DDD   DD   GGAG E♭DE♭C
kya- likheya kise   muqddr si----

DE♭G GG   GG GC'AG E♭D
httha diyaan char lkii-ra   da-

AAAA A AAA C'D'C' AG
tqdir   ta apni saukn si-,

C'C'C' D'C'AG C'   E♭'D'D'
tdbira sa-tho- na   hoiiyaan

C.AD DD DDD   D GG AGE♭DE♭C
na-- jng chhuteya na kn pa-te--,

DE♭G   GG   GG GG C'AG E♭D
 jhund langh gya inj hira- da-

AA   AA A AA AC'D'C' AG
mere git vi   lok suni-de- ne-,

C'C'   C'C'C' D'C'A GC'E♭'D' D'
nale kafir   aa-kh sdinde- ne

C.AD   DD D DD   GG AGE♭DE♭C
mai---   drd nu kaba kah bai-tha----,

DE♭ G GG GG   C'AG E♭D
rb   na rkh baitha pida- da-

A   AAAA   AC'D'C'AG   C'C'
mai dnashvra sunindiyaan-   sng

C'   C'C' D'C'AG C'E♭' D'D'
kaii vari uchchi- bol   piya

C.AD DD D DDD GGAG E♭DE♭C
kujh- man si sahnu ishke- da---

DE♭ GG G G C'AG E♭D
kujh dava vi si pida- da-

A AA A AAA C' D'C' AG
tu khud nu   aakl khnda- hain- ,

C'   C'C'   C' D'C'AG C'C'E♭'D' D'
mai khud   nu aa-shik dsda-   ha

C.AD   DD D GG AGE♭DE♭C
eh--   lokan te chhd daiiye-----,

D E♭ GG G GG   C'AG E♭D
kihnu man ne dende pira- da-

32. KINNA SONA TAINU RAB NE

Taal: Kaharwa Dugun
Transpose+1 and play from C Scale

Singer: Nusarat Fateh Ali
Chord: CE^{b}G   S=C#

kinna sona tainnu rab ne banaya, dil kare vekhda ravaan

kinna sona tainnu rab ne banaya

dil mudada nahin lakh samjhaya, dil kare vekhda ravaan

kinna sona tainnu rab ne banaya

pyar tera ae zindagi meri, karni ae main puja teri

meri zindagi da eho sadmaya, dil kare vekhda ravaan

kinna sona tainnu rab ne banaya

dil vich tera pyar vasa ke, vekhi javaan kol baitha ke

tainnu dil vaale shishe ch sajaaya, dil kare vekhda ravaan

kinna sona tainnu rab ne banaya

KINNA SONA TAINU RAB NE

dha	ge	n	ti	n	ke	dhi	n	dha	ge	n	ti	n	ke	dhi	n
1	2	3	4	5	6	7	8	1	2	3	4	5	6	7	8

E^{b}D   CC   CC   .A.A C   D .AE^b-D C
kinna sona tainnu   rb   ne bnaya

CD E^{b}F FE^{b}DE^b DC.A
dil   kre vekhda-   rva-

E^{b}D   CC   CC   .A.A E^b D CC
kinna sona tainnu   rb   ne bnaya

GG   GGG   G   GA   GFDE^b – DC
dil   murda   nii   lkh   smjhaya

CD   E^{b}F   FE^{b}DE^b DC.A
dil   kre   vekhda-   rva-

E^{b}D   CC CC   .A.A   E^b D   CC
kinna sona   tainnu   rb   ne   bnaya

GG   GA   A   GE^{b}G   AA
pyar tera ae zindgi meri

GAG   E^b D-G   E^{b}D   CC
krni   ae   mai-   puja teri

E^{b}D   CCC   C   .A.A CD.A E^b – DC
meri zindgi da   eho   sdmaya

CD   E^{b}F   FE^{b}DE^b DC.A
dil   kre   vekhda   rva-

E^{b}D   CC CC   .A.A   E^b D   CC
kinna sona   tainnu   rb   ne   bnaya

 G   GG   AA   GE^{b}G   GA   A
dil   vich tera   pyar   vsa ke

A G   E^{b}D-G   E^{b}D   CC   C
vekhii java   kol   baitha ke

E^{b}D   CC   CC   .A.A   C   D.AE^b—DC
tainnu dil   vale   shiishe ch   sjaya

CD   E^{b}F   FE^{b}DE^b DC.A
dil   kre   vekhda   rva-

E^{b}D   CC CC   .A.A   E^b D   CC
kinna sona   tainnu   rb   ne   bnaya

Vinod Kumar

33. KISE DA NAI KOI AITTHE YAAR

Film: Rang Le Dil Pyar Nal (1991)   Singer: Ataulla Khan
Taal: Kaharwa Dugun   Chord: GB^{b}D'   S=C

assaa es hayaati de din saare teri aas te inve guzaar di

sanu lagda hai auna koi nahin tu taiyon buhe udeek de mar ditte

khaida asa dahleez da chhadya na bade ruttaa ne sade te var kite

sir haad di dhup ne saad ditte hath oh de paale ne thaar ditte

kise da nahin koi aitthe yaar sare jhuthe ne

jhuthiyaan mohobbataan-2 te pyar sare jhuthe ne

jhuthe aitthe aashiqaa di aashiqi de rang ne

kachche dhage vaang aitthe sangiyaan de sang ne

kare koi kiddaan-2 aitbaar sare jhuthe ne

maali aitthe bagaan di bahaar vech dende ne

kaliyaan te fullaan da singar vech dende ne

karde ne pyar da-2 vyaapar sare jhuthe ne

oh ta ni jaan da ae jinnu yaar laggiyaan

pyar vaang dhokhebaaz kar de ne thagiyaan

soneyaa de kaul te qaraar sare jhuthe ne

har pase shuk di da dur taandi safni

thaao thaai sabnaa nu payi aapo apni

chor hon bhanve-2 pahredaar sare jhuthe ne

dukkhaan de ae kisse yaar sadika traat ne

heeraan ne farebi aetthe raanjhe dagabaz ne

pyar de ne jinne-2 thekedaar saare jhuthe ne

KISE DA NAI KOI AITTHE YAAR

dhage	nti	nke	dhin	dhage	nti	nke	dhin	dhage	nti	nke	dhin	dhage	nti	nke	dhin
12	34	56	78	12	34	56	78	12	34	56	78	12	34	56	78
G	A	A	B♭	B♭	A	A	G	E	-	A	A	G	G	G	-
ki	se	da	nii	ko	ii	ae	tthe	ya	-r	sa	re	jhu	the	ne	-
G	-A	B♭	D'	D'	E'	D'	E'	-	-	-	D'	D'	B♭	G	-
jhu	-thi	yaan	mo	ho	b	ta	-	-	-	-	-	-	-	-	-
G	A	B♭	D'	D'	E'	E'	D'	D'	-C'	C'	B	B	A	A	G
jhu	thi	yaan	mo	ho	b	ta	te	pya	-r	sa	re	jhu	the	ne	-

interlude: play sthayi.

dhage	nti	nke	dhin	dhage	nti	nke	dhin	dhage	nti	nke	dhin	dhage	nti	nke	dhin
D'	E'	E'	G'	G'	-F'	F'	E'	E'	E'	E'	F'	E'	D'	D'	-
jhu	the	ae	tthe	aa	-shi	kan	di	aa	shi	kii	de	rn	g	ne	-
D'	F'	E'	D'	C'	-B	G	A	B♭	B♭	A	A	G	G	G	-
k	chche	dha	ge	va	-g	ae	tthe	sn	gi	yaan	de	sn	g	ne	-
G	A	B♭	D'	D'	E'	D'	E'	-	-	-	-	-	-	-	-
k	re	ko	ii	ki	dda	-	-	-	-	-	-	-	-	-	-
D'	D'	C'	C'	B	B	A	G								
-	-	-	-	-	-	-	-								
G	A	B♭	D'	D'	E'	E'	D'	D'	-C'	C'	B	B	A	A	G
k	re	ko	ii	ki	dda	ae	t	ba	-r	sa	re	jhu	the	ne	-

interlude:

B♭B♭A G E GGA- B♭- A-

B♭-A B♭-A G E G-GB♭ A A A

B♭-A B♭-A G E G-GB♭ A G G

B♭ B♭ A B♭- A G E

B♭ B♭ A D' – C' B♭ A

E' D' C' B♭ A G B♭ D'

dhage	nti	nke	dhin	dhage	nti	nke	dhin	dhage	nti	nke	dhin	dhage	nti	nke	dhin
D'	E'	E'	G'	G'	-F'	F'	E'	E'	-E'	E'	-F'	E'	D'	D'	-
ma	li	ae	tthe	ba	ga	di	bi	ha	-r	ve	-ch	den	de	ne	-
D'	F'	E'	D'	C'	-B	G	A	B♭	-B♭	A	-A	G	G	G	-
k	li	yaan	te	fu	ll	da	sin	ga	-r	ve	-ch	den	de	ne	-

Vinod Kumar

| G | A | B♭ | D' | D' | E' | D' | E' | - | - | - | - | - | - | - | - |
| k | r | de | ne | pya | -r | da | - | - | - | - | - | - | - | - | - |

D'	D'	C'	C'	B	B	A	G

| G | A | B♭ | D' | D' | E' | E' | D' | D' | -C' | C' | B | B | A | A | G |
| k | r | de | ne | pya | -r | da | vya | pa | -r | sa | re | jhu | the | ne | - |

| G | A | A | B♭ | B♭ | A | A | G | E | - | A | A | G | G | G | - |
| ki | se | da | nii | ko | ii | ae | tthe | ya | -r | sa | re | jhu | the | ne | - |

interlude: as above.

| D' | E' | E' | G' | G' | -F' | F' | E' | E' | E' | E' | F' | E' | D' | D' | - |
| o | h | ta | nii | ja | n | da | e | ji | nnu | ya | r | l | gi | yaan | - |

| D' | -F' | E' | D' | C' | B | G | -A | B♭ | B♭ | A | A | G | G | G | - |
| pya | -r | va | ge | dho | khe | ba | -j | k | r | de | ne | th | gi | yaan | - |

| G | A | B♭ | D' | D' | E' | D' | E' | - | - | - | - | - | - | - | - |
| so | ne | yaan | de | kau | -l | te | - | - | - | - | - | - | - | - | - |

D'	D'	C'	C'	B	B	A	G

| G | A | B♭ | D' | D' | -E' | E' | D' | D' | -C' | C' | B | B | A | A | G |
| so | ne | yaan | de | kau | -l | te | k | ra | -r | sa | re | jhu | the | ne | - |

| G | A | A | B♭ | B♭ | A | A | G | E | - | A | A | G | G | G | - |
| ki | se | da | nii | ko | ii | ae | tthe | ya | -r | sa | re | jhu | the | ne | - |

34.   LANGH AA JA PATTAN

Album: Sada Vasda Rahe Punjab   Singer: Sudesh Kumari
Taal: Kaharwa   Chord: CFA   S=C#
Transpose+1 and play from C Scale
https://www.youtube.com/watch?v=6TSd_4D0KPM

langh aa ja pattan chanha da yaar, langh aa ja pattan chanha da
sir sadka main javan tere na da yaar,
langh aa ja pattan chanha da

mere kag banere te bolya, mera tatdi da divda doleya o
main taa mandadaa bol na boleya, -2 ho
langh aa ja pattan chanha da

ve main chadh kothe te khadiya, meriya sadiya paira diya taliya ve
jhulli hawa te zulfaan halliyaan, -2 ho
langh aa ja pattan chanha da

ve main rang suhe vich rangiyaa main ta lal dhole de mangiya ho
chahe changiya te chahe mandiya-2
langh aa ja pattan chanha da

Vinod Kumar

LANGH AA JA PATTAN

dha	ge	n	ti	n	ke	dhi	n	dha	ge	n	ti	n	ke	dhi	n
1	2	3	4	5	6	7	8	1	2	3	4	5	6	7	8

FF GF FB^{b}AG
o—o—o---- -2

prelude:
C'C'D'C' C'F'E^b'D' C'C'D'C' AB^{b}C'-
C'C'D'C' C'F'E^b'D' C'C'D'C' AB^{b}C'-
FF FGF FB^{b}AG FF FGF

FF FGF FB^{b}AG FF GF
o----------------------

 C   D   F   AAG AC'   B^b A F
langh aa ja pttn chnha da yar

AA   F   E^b DD.A .B^{b}C   C
lngh aa ja pttn   chnha   da

C   DDF   F   AA GA   C'   B^b A F
sir sdka   mai java tere na da yar

AA   F   E^b DD.A .B^{b}C   C
langh aa   ja pttn   chnha da

interlude:
C'C'C' E^b'D'C'B^{b}A FFAG F
C'C'C' E^b'D'C'B^{b}A FFAG F
B^{b}B^{b}B^{b}AG AAAGF GGGFD G-
FF GF nB^{b}AG FF GE^{b}F

FGE^b FA AAB^b A C'C'C'
mere- kag bnere te bolya

C'C'   GC'C' C' B^{b}B^{b}A C'C'B^b A
mera tatdi da divda   doleya o

A   G   FFE^b D.A   .B^b CCC
mai ta mndra bol   na   bolya

C   C   DDF   AG   A C'C'B^b A
mai ta mndra bol   na bolya o

AA   F   E^b DD.A .B^{b}C   C
lngh aa ja   pttn   chnha   da

F   FE^b E^b FA   B^{b}A   C'C'C'
ve mai-   chdh kothe te- khdiyaan

C'C'   C'C'   C'B^b AA   C'C'B^b A
meriyaan sdiyaan paira diyaan tliyaan   ve

AA   F   E^b DD.A .B^b CCC
jhulli hva te julfa-   hlliyaan

CC   D   F AAGA C'C'B^b A
jhulli hva te julfa-   hlliyaan ho

AA   F   E^b DD.A .B^{b}C   C
lngh aa ja   pttn   chnha   da

F   FE^b E^b FA   B^{b}A   C'C'C'
ve mai-   rng suhe vich rngiyaan

C'   C' C'   C'B^b A C'C'B^b A
mai ta lal dhole de mngiyaan ho

AA   FFE^b D .A .B^b CCC
chahe chngiyaan te chahe   mndiyaan

CC   DDF   A   GA   C'C'B^b
chahe chngiyaan te chahe   mndiyaan

AA   F   E^b DD.A .B^{b}C   C
lngh aa ja   pttn   chnha   da

Vinod Kumar

35. LATTHE DI CHAADAR

Lyrics: Shiv Kumar Batalvi   Singer: Bani aur Shivani
Taal: Kaharwa   Chord: CFA   S=C#
Transpose+1 and play from C Scale
https://youtu.be/0l0hMZuJgjA

latthe di chaadar utte saleti rang mahiya

aavo samne kolon di rus ke na langh mahiya

sadi kanda to mariya ae ankh ve

mere aate de vich hath ve

latthe di chaadar utte saleti rang mahiya

channa vekh ke n sade val hans ve

sadi ma payi karendiye shaq ve

latthe di chaadar utte saleti rang mahiya

gallaa goriyaa te kala kala til ve,

sada kad ke lai gaya dil ve

latthe di chaadar utte saleti rang mahiya

teri ma ne chadya saag ve,

asaa mangya te ditta ae jawab ve

latthe di chaadar utte saleti rang mahiya

teri ma ne chadiyan ae gandlaan,

asaa mangiya te pai gaiya dndlaa

latthe di chaadar utte saleti rang mahiya

teri ma ne pakaaiyaan ne rotiyaa

asaa mangiya te pai gaiya sotiyaa

latthe di chaadar utte saleti rang mahiya

teri ma ne pakaai ae kheer ve,
asaa mangi te pai gayi peed ve
latthe di chaadar utte saleti rang mahiya

teri ma de chitte chitte dand ve,
da lagya te devaa main bhann ve
latthe di chaadar utte saleti rang mahiya

teri ma di lambi sari gut ve,
da lagya te devaa main put ve
latthe di chaadar utte saleti rang mahiya

sade dil vich ki ki vasiyaan,
n tu puchhiya te n main dasiyaa
latthe di chaadar utte saleti rang mahiya

Vinod Kumar

LATTHE DI CHAADAR

dha	ge	n	ti	n	ke	dhi	n	dha	ge	n	ti	n	ke	dhi	n
1	2	3	4	5	6	7	8	1	2	3	4	5	6	7	8

prelude aur interlude tune: CC DF AG AG, CC DF GF GF

FGF G AGF FGF GAG DD   DDE-DC
ltthe- di chadr utte- sleti rng   mahiya

CC   DFF   FG   G AA   G F DF   FFF
aavo samne kolo   di rus ke n lng   mahiya

FG   AA   A AAA A GG   G-F FG   A-A A AA   GG G-F
sadi knda to mriya e ankh ve, mere aa-te de vich hth ve

ltthe di chadr utte sleti rng mahiya.....

FG   AA   A A AA AA GG G-F FG   A   A   AA   A GG G-F
chnna vekh ke n sade vl hns ve,   sadi man pi krendi ye shk ve

ltthe di chadr utte sleti rng mahiya.....

FG A AA   A AA   AA GG G-F FG AA A A AA A GG G-F
gll goriyaan te kala kala til ve,   sada kd ke le gya e dil   ve

ltthe di chadr utte sleti rng mahiya....

play rest of the song as above.

36. MAAI DE BHAWAN TE

Durga Mata Bhajan
Lyrics: Darshi
Singer: Narendra Chanchal
Transpose -1 and play from C Scale
https://wynk.in/music

Chord: CE^{b}G   S=B
Taal: Kaharwa

maai de bhawan te fullan di barkha

o ho rahi jai jai kaar bhawan te fullan di barkha

bhagtaa ne fullaa diyaa thaaliyaa sajaaiyaa ne

chandi deeyaa kauliyaa ch jotaan jagaaiyaa ne

jhum rahe masti vich sare, dati tere lal piyare

ban ke sevadar bhawan te fullan di barkha

maiya de dware aj raunkaa ne badiyaa

lambiyaa kataaraa vich sangtaa ne khadiyaa

har paase gunjan jaikaare baithe daati khol dware

bhar dendi bhandaar bhawan te fullaan di barkha

chandan di chauki te aasan lagaa leya

bhola bhala rup meri maai ne banaa laiya

lal lal choleyaan vaali bhar dendi hai jholi khali

bhar dendi bhandaar bhawan te fullaan di barkha

lahar vich aay maiya khushiyaa lutaanwadi

daya vaale hatthaan naal khairaan paii paanwadi

nirbal nu balwaan banaave murakh nu gunwaan banaave

'darshi' kare pukaar bhawan te fullan di barkha

Vinod Kumar

MAAI DE BHAWAN TE

dha	ge	n	ti	n	ke	dhi	n	dha	ge	n	ti	n	ke	dhi	n
1	2	3	4	5	6	7	8	1	2	3	4	5	6	7	8

prelude aur interlude: CDC DE^{b}D CDC .B
CDC DE^{b}D CDC C

CD D CDE^b E^b DD D CC
maii de bhvn te fulla di brkha

G F F F F E DDE^b E^b DD D CC
o ho rii jai jai kar bhvn te fulla di brkha

DEE E EE EE DEE EEE E
bhgta ne fulla diyaan thaliyaan sjaiiyaan ne

CD DD DDC D ED CCC C
chandi diyaan kauliyaan ch jota jgaiiyaan ne

F FF FF FF FF FF FF DF FFF
jhum rhe msti vich sare, dati tere lal piyare

G A GFE DDE^b E^b DD D CC
bn ke sevadar bhvn te fulla di brkha

EE E EEE EE DEE E EEE
maiiya de dvare aj raunkan ne badiyaan

CDD DDD CD EED D CCC
lmbiyaan ktara vich sngta ne khdiyaan

F FF FF FFF FF FF DF FFF
hr pase gunjn jaikare, baithi dati khol dvare

G AG F E DDE^b E^b D D D CC
bhr dendi bhndar bhvn te fulla di brkha

EE E EE E DE EE EE
chndn di chokii te aasn lga laiya

```
CD   DD   DD   CD   E   D   CC   CC
bhola bhala rup meri maii ne bna laiya


F   F   FFF        FF   F  FF    F  DF    FF
lal  lal  choleyaan vali,  bhr dendi hai  jholi  khali


G   AG   FE    DDEᵇ  Eᵇ   DD   D   CC
bhr dendi bhndar bhvn    te   fulla di  brkha


EE  E   EE  EE    DEE       EEEE
lhr vich aay  maiya khushiyaan lutanvdi


DD   DD   DD   CD  EE    D  CCC
dya  vale httha  nal khaira paii pavdi


 F F   F  F F   FFF      FF    F   F DF   FFF
nirbl  nu  blvan bnave,  murkh  nu  gunvan bnave


 G A   GF  EE    DDEᵇ  Eᵇ  D D  D  CC
"drshii"  kre pukar bhvn    te   fulla di  brkha
```

37. MANN JA BALMA

Taal: Kaharwa   Singer: Surinder Kaur, Asa
Transpose+2 and play from C Scale   Singh Mastana
                                       Chord: DFA   S=D
https://www.youtube.com/watch?v=vyT8onvLMEI
lau ji sajjano es geet nu zara dhyan naal suno

o.... ve mann ja baalma -2

mann ja baalma kyun gussa chadyai oye

ve mastaneya, ve rud pud jaaneya kyun butha sadyai oye

o faishan vekh ke ulta tera ni

kurta paat gaya gusse vich mera ni

Vinod Kumar

o.. main sandal o laine jede uchchi addi de
chal bazar challan nai gusse kaddi de
mann ja baalma

ve sajjan jande ne jado janaani saindal mange
din change nai, eho jaye vele ki karna e

oye jutti o laini oye meriye bhambiiriye
oye jutti o laini jedi rabad di labbe nii
sir vich vajje te koi satt na lagge ni

o…ye… ve shahar bambai vichcho mainu pars manga de ve
sineme main jana, ve sineme main jana vich paise pa de ve
mann ja baalma
lo ji jadon pars mange janani, te kurta pata hoye te ki kahna ae
pate kurte di tu gutthi sava lai ni
aa lai aanne do vich chhole pa lai ni

o… ye… main saari o laini jedi hove naylan di
o teri meri ve gal maaiyaan taan bandi
mann ja baalma

saari khaddad di tainnu pindon mangaan daanga
jad o paat gayi main kachchhe sawa laanga

MANN JA BALMA

dha	ge	n	ti	n	ke	dhi	n	dha	ge	n	ti	n	ke	dhi	n
1	2	3	4	5	6	7	8	1	2	3	4	5	6	7	8

lau ji sjjno aes git nu zra dhyan nal suno

prelude v interlude tune:
DD EE FF EE DD FF E- AAA
DD EE FF EE DD FF E-

G – F$^{\#}$ G—F$^{\#}$ G – F – E-
o………………………………

D F F EEE D F F EEE D
ve mnn ja balma ve mnn ja balma-

F F EEE D FF EE G
mnn ja balma kyu gussa chdhyaii oye

F FEEED F F F EEE D FF EE E
ve mstaneyaan, ve rur mur janeyaan kyu butha sryaii oye

B BBB BB B BC' BA A
o faishn vekh ke ulta tera ni

FF EE EE DF FF EE G
kurta pat gya gusse vich mera ni

FF EE EE DF FF EE E
kurta pat gya gusse vich mera ni

D E FEFE D FF E EE DD FF EE G
o.. mai saindl o lene jede uchchi addi de

D F F E ED D FF EE E
ve chl bazar chll naii gusse kddi de

F F EEE
mnn ja balma

Vinod Kumar

ve   sjjn   jande ne jdon jnani saindl mnge
din chnge naii, eho jye vele kii krna e

 B   BB   B BB   B   C'C'B   AGG A-
oye jutti o leni   ni, meriye   bhmbiriye

B   BB B BB   BB BC' C' BA   A
o   jutti o leni jedi rbr di lbbe ni

G   F   EE E   DD   FF   F EE   E
sir vich vjje te koii   stt   n lgge ni

 G- F# G- A- GFE-
o..ye....
D   F   FE   EE   DD   FF   FE   E   G
ve shhr bmbaii vichcho mainu prs manga de ve

D FF   E   EED
ve sineme mai jana,

D   FF   E   EE   D   FF   E   E E
ve saneme mai jana vich paise pa de ve

F   F EEE
mnn ja balma

lau ji jdon prs mnge jnani, te kurta pata hoe,
te kii kaina e

BC'   BB   B B   BB   BC' B A
pate kurte di tu gutthi sva lai ni

 G F EE   E   DD   FF   E   E E
aa lai aanne do vich chhole pa lai ni

D E D E D   FF   E   EE   DD   FF   EE   G
o ye ..   mai sari   o laini jedi hove nayln di

FF   EE E D   FF   E   EE
teri meri ve gl maiiyaan ta bndi

```
F    F    EEE
mnn  ja   balma

C'C' BB    B  BB    BC'    BA   A   A
sadi khddr di tainnu pindo mnga dan ga

 GG  F EE EE D    FF      FE  E  E
jd   o pat gayi mai kchchhe sva lan ga -2
```

(you can play many punjabi songs on this tune)

38. MATTHE TE CHAMKAN WAL

Lok Geet
Taal: Kaharwa Dugun
Transpose+2 and play from C Scale
https://youtu.be/FNVsnjeTDGM

Singer: Musarrat Nazir
Chord: CE^{b}G   S=D

matthe te chamkan vaal
matthe te chamkan vaal, mere banre de

laao ni lao aenu shagnaa di mehndi-2
mehndi kare hath laal, mere banre de
matthe te chamkan vaal, mere banre de

paao ni paao aenu shagnaa da gaanna-2
gaanne de rang ne kamaal, mere banre de
matthe te chamkan vaal, mere banre de

aaiyaan ni aaiyaan bhaina mehndi lae ke
bhaina nu kinne ne khayaal, mere banre de
matthe te chamkan vaal, mere banre de

(on the same tune you can sing mitthe lagde guruji tere bol vele
amrat de)

Vinod Kumar

MATTHE TE CHAMKAN WAL

dha	ge	n	ti	n	ke	dhi	n	dha	ge	n	ti	n	ke	dhi	n
1	2	3	4	5	6	7	8	1	2	3	4	5	6	7	8

E^{b}E^b E^b E^{b}F   E^b D^b D^{b}E^{b}CD^b E^{b}FGA^b GE^{b}FD^b E^b
bhaina nu kinne ne khya---l   me-re- bnre de

E^b E^b E^b E^{b}FE^{b}D^b D^{b}E^{b}CD^b E^{b}FGA^b GE^{b}FD^b E^b
mtthe te chmkn   va---l,   me-re- bnre- de

39. MERA IS JAG VICH KOI NA

Taal: Kaharwa
Transpose+1 and play from C Scale

Singer: Mahinder Raj, Neelam Sahni and others
Chord: CEG   S=C#

https://wynk.in/music

jagdamba he ma, mera is jag vich koi na, <u>he jagdambe ma</u>-2

har pal tera naam jappaa, <u>he jagdambe ma</u>-2

tu hai mata mamtamayi, mamtamayi ma mamtamayi

o kaun dayalu tere jayi ma, tere jayi ma tere jayi

santa te teri thandi chhaan, <u>he jagdambe ma</u>-2

tere mandaraan vich sukh milde, sukh milde ma sukh milde

aashaa vale ful khilde ma, ful khilde ma ful khilde

rakh ma nazraan mehar diyaan, <u>he jagdambe ma</u>-2

tu ma bede paar kare, paar kare ma paar kare

o taap hare santaap hare ma, taap hare, santaap hare taap hare

aprampaar teri mahima, <u>he jagdambe ma</u>-2

Vinod Kumar

MERA IS JAG VICH KOI NA

dha	ge	n	ti	n	ke	dhi	n	dha	ge	n	ti	n	ke	dhi	n
1	2	3	4	5	6	7	8	1	2	3	4	5	6	7	8

FGAC'C'D' G A
jgdmba he ma

DE FE DE FE DEFE D- C-
mera is jg vich ko-ii- na------,

C DDEE D-EDEDC C DDEE D
he jgdmbe ma--------- he jgdmbe ma

DE FE DEFE DEF ED-C-
hr pl te-ra- na-m jpa----

C DDEE D-EDEDC C DDEE D
he jgdmbe ma--------- he jgdmbe ma

F# F# F#F# EF#G GF#
tu hai mata mmta myi,

EF#G GF# F# EF#G GF#
mmta myi ma mmta myi

B BB BBAABDb' ABA AbA D
o kaun dya—lu-- tere- jyi ma,

DE GF# E DE GF# ED DD
tere jyi ma tere jyi tere jyi

DEFE DE FE DEFE D-C-
sn-ta- te- teri thn-di- chha

C DDEE D-EDEDC C DDEE D
he jgdmbe ma--------- he jgdmbe ma

(play rest as above)

40. NI MAIN NACHNA MOHAN DE NAL

Krishna Bhajan   Chord: F$^{\#}$AD$^{b\prime}$ S=C#
Taal: Kaharwa Dugun
Transpose+1 and play from C Scale
https://youtu.be/LM9btYaT0bM

ni main nachna mohan de naal aaj mainu nach lain de

nach lain de ni mainu nach lain de

ni main nach ke manana dildaar aaj mainu nach lain de

duniya de layi nacheya bathera, fir vi na koi banya mera

ki karna, jai ho, ki karna jaiho

ki karna hai ae sansaar aaj mainu nach lain de

ni main nachna mohan de naal aaj mainu nach lain de

pairaan de vich ghungru bann ke, apne shyam di jogan ban ke

ni main nach ke, jai ho, ni main nach ke, jai ho,

ni main nach ke manana nandlaal aaj mainu nach lain de

ni main nachna mohan de naal aaj mainu nach lain de

satguru ne ae rasta dikhaya, banke bihaari ton mainu milaya

aise satguru te aise satguru te

aise satguru te main balihaar aaj mainu nach lain de

ni main nachna mohan de naal aaj mainu nach lain de

vrindavan vich jaavan de lai, pyar mohan da paavan de lai

sune banwari ne sune banwari ne

sune banwari ne taane hazaar aaj mainu nach lain de

Vinod Kumar

NI MAIN NACHNA MOHAN DE NAL

dhage	nti	nke	dhin	dhage	nti	nke	dhin	dhage	nti	nke	dhin	dhage	nti	nke	dhin
12	34	56	78	12	34	56	78	12	34	56	78	12	34	56	78

prelude:
F$^{\#}$ A F$^{\#}$ E F$^{\#}$-A-AAA, F$^{\#}$ A F$^{\#}$ E F$^{\#}$-A-AAA
F$^{\#}$ A F$^{\#}$ E F$^{\#}$-AAC'BA, F$^{\#}$ A F$^{\#}$ E F$^{\#}$-A-AAA
D'AB - B D'C'A, ABF$^{\#}$ AC'- B- AA-
AAA AF$^{\#}$A BC'BC', B--- BD$^{b'}$ D$^{b'}$ D$^{b'}$
BD$^{b'}$ BA A

A A   EF$^{\#}$F$^{\#}$A E' E' A A   EF$^{\#}$F$^{\#}$A E' E'
ni main nachna jy ho ni main nachna jy ho   A A
                                                                       ni mai

E F$^{\#}$F$^{\#}$ A A | A - BC'BC' | B - - B | D$^{b'}$ D$^{b'}$ D$^{b'}$ D$^{b'}$
n chna - mo | hn - de- -- | na - - l | a j mai nu

B D$^{b'}$ B A | A - - - | D$^{b'}$ E' E' E' | F$^{\#'}$ F$^{\#'}$ F$^{\#'}$ F$^{\#'}$
n ch lai n | de - - - | n ch lai n | de ni mai nu

B C' B C' | B A A A | E F$^{\#}$F$^{\#}$ A E' | E' - A A
n ch lai n | de - ni mai | n chke - jy | ho - ni mai

E F$^{\#}$F$^{\#}$ A E' | E' - A A | E F$^{\#}$F$^{\#}$ A A | A A C' -
n chke - jy | ho - ni mai | n chke - m | na na dil -

B - - - | D$^{b'}$ D$^{b'}$ D$^{b'}$ D$^{b'}$ | B D$^{b'}$ B A | A - A A
da - - r | a j mai nu | n ch lai n | de - ni mai

E F$^{\#}$F$^{\#}$ A A | A - BC'BC' | B - - B | D$^{b'}$ D$^{b'}$ D$^{b'}$ D$^{b'}$
n chna - mo | hn - de- -- | na - - l | a j mai nu

B D$^{b'}$ B A | A - - - |
n ch lai n | de - - - |

interlude:
E' E' E' F$^{\#'}$ E' F$^{\#'}$ E'-
C' C' C' B A B A-
E F$^{\#}$ A E' D$^{b'}$---
C' C' C' B A B A-

												E'	E'	E'
												du	ni	ya
F#'	-	F#'	-	B	C'	B	C'	A	B	B	A	-	E'	E'	E'
de	-	l	ii	n	ch	ya	b	the	-	ra	-	-	fi	r	vi
E'	F#'	F#'	-	B	C'	B	C'	A	B	B	A	E'	D'	C'D'	B
na	-	ko	ii	b	n	ya	-	me	-	ra	-	-	-	-	-
A	-	A	-	E	F#F#	A	E'	E'	-	A	-	E	F#F#	A	E'
-	-	kii	-	k	rna	-	jy	ho	-	kii	-	k	rna	-	jy
E'	-	A	-	E	F#F#	A	A	A	-	C'	-	B	-	-	B
ho	-	kii	-	k	rna	-	hai	ae	-	sn	-	sa	-	-	r
Db'	Db'	Db'	Db'	B	Db'	B	A	A	-	A	A	E	F#F#	A	A
a	j	mai	nu	n	ch	lai	-n	de	-	ni mai		n	chna	-	mo
A	-	BC'BC'		B	-	-	B	Db'	Db'	Db'	Db'	B	Db'	B	A
hn	-	de-	--	na	-	-	l	a	j	mai nu		n	ch	lai	n
A	-	-	-
de	-	-	-

```
E'E'     E'F#'  F#'F#'  BC'BC'        AB  BA
paira   de-    vich    ghunghru-     bnn ke-,

E'E'E'   E'F#'F#'   F#' BC'BC'  AB  BA
apne     shyam      di  jo-gn   bn  ke-,

music: E' D' C'D'B- A

A A    EF# F#A     E'  E'  A  A  EF# F#A  E'  E'
ni mai nch ke-,    jy  ho, ni mai nch ke-,  jy  ho,

A A    EF#    F#A  A F# A  BC'B-  Db'Db'  Db'Db'  BDb'  BA  A
ni mai nch    ke- mnana  nndlal  aaj     mainu   nch   lain de

A A    EF#F#A    AA   BC'BC'  BB  D'D'  D'D'  BD'  BA  A
ni mai nchna-    mohn de-------  nal aaj mainu nch lain  de
```

Vinod Kumar

E'E'E'E'   F#' F#'   BC'B   C'ABBA
stguru   ne   ae   rasta dikha-ya-,

E'E'   E'E'F#'F#'   F#' BC'B   C'ABBA
banke biha-ri   to mai-nu   mila-ya-

AA   EF#F#A   A   AA   EF#F#A   A
aese stguru   te aese stguru   te

AA   EF#F#A   A   A BC'B- Db'Db'   Db'Db' BDb' BA A
aese stguru   te mai blihar aaj   mainu nch lain de

A A   EF#F#A   AA   BC'BC' BB Db'Db' Db'Db'   BDb' BA A
ni mai nchna-   mohn de------- nal aaj   mainu nch lain de

E'E'E'F#'   F#'F#' BC'BC' AB BA'
vrindavn   vich   ja-vn   de- laii,

AB   BA   E'   E'E'F#'   F#' BC'BC
pyar mohn da   pa-vn   de- laii

AA   E-F#A   A AA   E-F#A   A
sune ban-vri ne sune ban-vri   ne

AA   E-F#A   A AB C'B- Db'Db'   Db'Db'   BDb' BA A
sune ban-vri ne tane hjar aaj   mainu   nch   lain de

A A   EF#F#A   AA   BC'BC' BB D'D' D'D' BD' BA A
ni mai nchna-   mohn de------- nal aaj mainu nch lain de

41. NIT KHAIR MANGA SONEYA

Taal: Kaharwa
Transpose+1 and play from C Scale

Music: Nusarat Fateh Ali
Singer: Nusarat Fateh Ali
Chord: CFA   S=C#

https://www.youtube.com/watch?v=f-s4mM9ls8o

hor ki mangana main rab kolo, nit khair mangaa main tere dam di
baaj sajan lajpal tere, main khojiyaan kede kam di
pal pal maneya sukh ve hazaraa ghadi vekhe n koi alam di
badar hamesha maula rakhe dhola, tain te nazar karam di

nit khair manga soneya main teri, dua na koi hor mangdi
tere pairaanch akheer hove meri, dua na koi hor mangdi

dam dam khair kare rab teri manga roz main sajan duavaa
sadka tera main ae zindadi lakh vaari dhol ghumaanvaa
peer shabbir da sadka dhola, tainnu lagan na garam hawawa
jug jug jiiven shala tu teri aayi main mar jaawaan

tere pyar ditta jadon da sahara ve,
mainu bhul gaya maahiya jag saara ve
khushi eho mainnu sajna batheri, dua na koi hor mangdi

tu milya te mil gayi khudayi ve, hath jod aakha panvi na judayi ve
mar javangi je ankh maittho feri, dua na koi hor mangdi

pawaan vasta ve kalli chhad javin na,
hassa mainu kitte jag da banayi na
shala jhulle na judayi di haneri, dua na koi hor mangdi

Vinod Kumar

NIT KHAIR MANGA SONEYA

dha	ge	n	ti	n	ke	dhi	n	dha	ge	n	ti	n	ke	dhi	n
1	2	3	4	5	6	7	8	1	2	3	4	5	6	7	8

C   C   CC   C   C CDC.B♭ .B♭   .B♭C   CD   C.B♭ C   C
hor kii mngna mai rb kolo---,   nit khair mnga tere dm di

CC .B♭C CCC CDC.B♭   .B♭   .B♭CD   C.B♭   C   C
baj sjn ljpal tere------, mai khojiyaan kede km di

G FD FD   CC C CCD-C.B♭ .B♭.B♭ CC   C DD .B♭C C
pl pl mneya sukh ve hzara,   ghdi vekhe n koii alm di

GGF DFD   DD   DD DD   F   D DDD CC   C
bdr   hmesha maula rkhe dhola, tain te nzr   krm di

CC DF   DC   DFD C   DC
nit khair mnga soneya mai   teri

.B♭.B♭   C DF DC CCC
duaa na koii hor mngdi

FF   GGG   GFB♭ AG   FD
tere pairanch akhiir hove meri

.B♭.B♭ C DF DC CCC
duaa na koii hor mngdi

GG FD FD DD C.B♭ CD .B♭.B♭   DD D DDC .B♭CC
dm dm khair kre rb   teri   mnga roj mai sjn duaava

DDD DD D D CCD-C.B♭ .B♭.B♭ CC   DD .B♭CC
sdka tera mai ae jindni----- lkh vari dhol ghumanva

DC CDD C DDD CD-C.B♭   .B♭.B♭ CCC C DDC .B♭CC
pir shbbir da sdka dhola-----, tainnu   lgn na grm hvava

GG GG GG GG G FG B♭B♭ G FD FF
jug jug jiven shala tu teri aaii mai mr java

```
FF  G     GG   GG   A  B♭GA    A---G
tere  pyar  ditta  jdon  da  sahara  ve-----

GG      C'C'    AG    AA        GF   GG  F-DCD
mainnu  bhul   gya  mahiyaan  jg     sara  ve-------

CC      DF    DC      DFD   CDC
khushii  eho  mainnu  sjna     btheri

.B♭.B♭   C  DF   DC  CCC
duaa   na  koii  hor   mngdi

F   FGG  G  GG   A   B♭GA    AG
tu  milya  te   mil  gaii  khudaii  ve-

GG  C'   AG     AA   G  FGG  F-DCD
hth  jor  aakhan  pavi  na  judaii  ve

CC   DFD   C  DF   DC      DC
mr    javagi  je  ankh  maittho  feri

.B♭.B♭    C  DF   DC  CCC
duaa   na  koii  hor   mngdi

FF   GGG  G  GG   AB♭  GA   A--G
pava  vasta  ve  klli  chhd  javin  na

GG      C'C'     AG   AA   G  FGG     F-DCD
hassa  mainnu   kitte   jg  da  bnayi      na

CC     DF   D  CDF       D  CDC
shala  jhulle  na  judaiiyaan  di  hneri

.B♭.B♭  C  DF   DC   CCC
duaa   na  koii   hor   mngdi
```

Vinod Kumar

42. PANDIT JI AE BAL MERA

Taal: Kaharwa   Singer: Surinder Kaur, Asa Singh
Mastana
Chord: EGB   S=C
https://www.youtube.com/watch?v=Ceg55Md_xp8

pandatji ae bal mera-2 ma pyo da naam chamkaayega
partap shivaji vaangu ki ae bharat veer kahavega
ae munda nira shanishchar ee din raat pawade paayega
onde jaande nu chhedega bhaiye da sir fadwayega

dhan di kothi te chandra su ya paise vi kuj khattega
dhan kidron kidron auna ae ki sona veche vattega
mai tu dhan bare puchheya ee, par patari kuj aedaan dasdi ae
ki dasdi ae pandat ji
ae ghar de bhande vechega daaru di botal vattega
pardesaan da dhan likhiya ae station te kheese kattega

kinni koi vidya pauni ae kinni ko tarakki karni ae
ki vadda afsar bane main sadraan di jholi bharni ae
ae kain sitare vidya de ae chann navaan hi chadega
kad chaaku naklaan teepega dhid mastaraan de paadega

vyah da vi lekha la vekho othe ki lekh likhaaye ne
is raje de ghar sone jaye rab ne sanjog milaaye ne
maai tun vyah baare puchheya ee, haan pandat ji
par patri kuj aedaan dasdi ae, kii dasdi ae pandat ji

darh vatt zamana kat bibi aetthe vi ghale male ne
do vyah patri vich likkhe ne do tabbar dubban vale ne

pandat ji mera puttar aeda bhaira nahin jiddaan tusi kainde paye
ho,   ma jo hoiyon

karmaan da bhaida hovega aklaan da kachcha hovega

o kuj vi hai ae pandat ji par dil da sachcha hovega

ae dil da sachcha hovega na bhedbhav nu mannega

ae hindu muslim sikh isaayi sabde chandare bhannega

ki neki koyi kamaayega ki bhukheyaan taai khawayega

aenna te dasso pandatji ae baahar vi kidre jaayega

teri murad pukarn to hai bibi, haan pandat ji

par patari kuj aedaan dasdi ae

bhukheyaan to kho ke khaayega, hadtaalaan roz karaayega

ae baahar jaan de yog nahin chheti andar ho jaayega

o bhatke hoye jawano ae ki fad laye chaale hosh karo

chand de ghar vi ja panhuche ne aaj duniyawalon hosh karo

saun bhagat singh di kha ke te bas aaj aenna hi kahna hai

na rolo deep jawani nu ae bharat ma da kahna hai

Vinod Kumar

PANDIT JI AE BAL MERA

dha	ge	n	ti	n	ke	dhi	n	dha	ge	n	ti	n	ke	dhi	n
1	2	3	4	5	6	7	8	1	2	3	4	5	6	7	8

prelude:

(EGB) x 6

$D^{b'}$ $D^{b'}$ $D^{b'}$ $D^{b'}$- $D^{b'}$ A   B B B B- B G

A A A A- A F G- G- F-

EFGF FFFF AA GG AAAA

EFGF FFFF AA GG FFFF   (A)

$D^{b'}$ D' $D^{b'}$ B A G F E F -

FE   F G   G F   FFE

pndt ji kii ae bal mera -

FE F G   G F   FF   F   F   F G   FFFF

pndt ji kii ae bal mera man pyo da na chmkayega

music: AA GG FF FF

 FEF   F G F FF   F B AAA GG GFFF

prtap   shivaji vagu kii ae bhart vir khavega

music: F-G-A-B- $D^{b'}$- D'- $D^{b'}$- (K)

$D^{b'}$ $D^{b'}$$D^{b'}$ $D^{b'}$$D'$ $D^{b'}$$D^{b'}$$D^{b'}$ $D^{b'}$ $D^{b'}$ $D^{b'}$$D'$ $D^{b'}$BB AB B

ae munda nira shnishchr   ii din   rat   pvade payega

AA   AA   A   AA A   FE   F G   FFFF

aunde jande nu chhedega bhaiye da sir fadvayega

music:

EFGF FFFF AA GG AAAA

EFGF FFFF AA GG FFFF

$D^{b'}$ D' $D^{b'}$ B A G F E F -

A   A A A   A BBA   A A^{b}F A^b A
dhn di kothi   te chndra su

A   A   A A A BBA   A A   BA   A AA   BAA
dhn di kothi te chndra su ya paise vi kuj khttega

F   EEF   GGF FF   F B AA   GG   FFF (K)
dhn kidro   kidro auna e kii sona veche vttega

music: F- G- A- B-
maii tu dhn bare puchheya ii, pr ptri kuj eda dsdi e
kii dsdi e pndt ji---

D$^{b'}$ B D$^{b'}$ D$^{b'}$D$^{'}$ BD$^{b'}$D$^{b'}$ D$^{b'}$D$^{b'}$ D$^{'}$ D$^{b'}$ B   ABB
ae ghr de bhande vechega daru di   botal   vattega

A A^b A   A   A   A^b A^b A A   F E   F GF   FFF   (A)
prdesan da dhn likhiya   e, steshn te khiise kttega

AA   A   AAA   BA   A D$^{b'}$ D$^{'}$ B A G F -
kinni koii vidya pauni e

AA   A   AAA   BA   A AA   A AAA   BA   A
kinni koii vidya pauni e kinni ko trkki   krni   e

F   EF GGF   FF B   BBA A GG   FF   F (K)
kii vdda afsr   bne mai sdra di jholi bhrni e

D$^{b'}$ D$^{b'}$D$^{b'}$ D$^{b'}$D$^{b'}$D$^{b'}$ D$^{b'}$D$^{b'}$D$^{b'}$ D$^{b'}$ D$^{b'}$ D$^{b'}$D$^{b'}$ D$^{b'}$B B ABB
ae kain   sitare   vidya   de ae chnn   nva hi chadega

AA A^{b}A   A^{b}A^{b}A A^{b}AA   FF   EFG   F FFF (A)
kd chaku nkla   tipega dhid mastra de padega

A   A^b A AA   B AA – A^{b}F A^b A -
vyah da vi lekha la vekho

A   A A AA^b B AA   AA A AA A^{b}BA   A
vyah da vi lekha la vekho othe kii lekh likhae ne

FF EF G   F   FF   B BB A AGG   GFF   F (K)
is   raje de ghr sone jai rb ne snjog milaye ne

maii tu vyah bare puchheya ii,   ha pndt ji
pr ptri kuj   eda dsdi e, kii dsdi e pndt ji—

D$^{b’}$D$^{b’}$ D$^{b’}$D$^{b’}$ D$^{b’}$D$^{b’}$D’ D$^{b’}$D$^{b’}$ D$^{b’}$D$^{b’}$ D$^{b’}$D$^{b’}$ D’ BB   AB   B
dr   vtt   zmana kt   bibi etthe vi ghale male ne

A A^b AAA^b AA A^{b}A A F EEE FGF   FF   F
do vyah ptri vich likkhe ne do tbbr   dubbn vale ne

pndt ji mera puttr aeda bhaida nhi jidda tusi kainde pye
ho….   man jo hoiyo

AA   A AA   BAA D$^{b’}$ D’ B A G F
krman da bhaida hovega

AA   A AA   BAA   AA A AA   BAA
krman da bhaida hovega akla da kchcha hovega

F EE F G F FFF B B A A GG   FFF (K)
jo kuj vi hai ae pndt ji pr dil da schcha hovega

D$^{b’}$ D$^{b’}$ D$^{b’}$ D$^{b’}$D’ BD$^{b’}$D$^{b’}$ D$^{b’}$ D$^{b’}$D’D$^{b’}$B B ABB
ae dil da schcha hovega na bhedbhav nu mnnega

A A^{b}A   A^{b}A^b A A^b A AA^{b}A EEE FFG   FFF (A)
ae hindu muslim sikkh iisaii sbde chndre bhnnnega

A AA AA A^{b}BAA D$^{b'}$ D' B A G F
kii nekii koii kmaega

A AA AA A^{b}BAA A AAA   A A^{b}BAA
kii nekii koii kmaega kii bhukheyaan taii khvayega

FE F GF FFF B B A A GGG FFF (K)
enna te dsso pndt ji ae bahr vi kidre jaega

teri murad pukarn to hai bibi, ha pndt ji
pr ptri kuj eda dsdi e—

 BD$^{b'}$D$^{b'}$ D$^{b'}$ D$^{b'}$ D' BD$^{b'}$D$^{b'}$ D$^{b'}$D$^{b'}$D' BB BABB
bhukheyaan to kho ke khayega, hrtala   roz kraega

A A AA A AA AA FE   FG F FFF (A)
ae bahr jan de yog nhi chheti andr ho jaega

pndt ji koii ray pan da rah dsso
achchha jis trh bibi tu kinni e

D$^{b'}$ BBD$^{b'}$ D$^{b'}$D$^{b'}$ D'D$^{b'}$D$^{b'}$ D$^{b'}$ D$^{b'}$ D$^{b'}$ D' BB AB BB
o bhtke hoe jvano   ae kii far lye chale hosh kro

A A^{b}A^{b}A A A^{b}BA A A B A AA BA AA
o bhtke hoe jvano ae kii far lye chale hosh kro

F E F G F FF   B B BAA GG FF FF
chnd de ghr vi ja pnhuche ne aj duniya valo hosh kro

 A AAA AA A B A A AA BA A AA BA A
so bhgt sinh di kha ke te bs enna hi aj kaina hai

F EF GF FFF B B AAA G G FF F
na raulo dip jvani nu ae bhart man da kaina hai.

Vinod Kumar

43. SANU IK PAL CHAIN NA AAVE

Taal: Kaharwa

Singer: Nusarat Fateh Ali
Chord: FAC'   S=C

https://youtu.be/2yzxRN2o9ds

sanu ik pal chain na aave-2 sajna tere bina o sajna tere bina
sada kalyaan ji nahiyon lagna-2 sajna tere bina o sajna tere bina

raati main jalaawaan deeva hanjuaan de tel da
hay o rabba sajna nu chheti kyun nahin melda
sanu ik pal chain na aave…

kise da yaar na pardes jaave
vichhoda na kise de pesh aave
sanu ik pal chain na aave…..

rog viyog te sog hazaraan sajnaa tere naa de
ho na bhaandi roz qayamat vichhde yaar jinnaan de
sanu ik pal chain na aave….

o kaga tainnu churiyaan paavaan kadi saade vi baith banere
leve naam koi sajnaa vaala te main sagan manaavaan tere
sanu ik pal chain na aave…

SANU IK PAL CHAIN NA AAVE

dha	ge	n	ti	n	ke	dhi	n	dha	ge	n	ti	n	ke	dhi	n
1	2	3	4	5	6	7	8	1	2	3	4	5	6	7	8

```
AA    AA   A  AG   A   FG
sanu ek  pl chain na aave -2


DGG   FF FF –D    D   D GG  FF  FF
sjna   tere bina      o  sjna   tere bina


FG   AC'C'  C'   D'D'    C'D'D'C'
sada klya  ji  nhiyo   lgna- -2


F'F'F'    F'F'  D'D'C'G   GGG  FF  FF
sjna      tere    bina      sjna tere bina


AA  A  AA^bA   AA   A AG   F  GG C' A G
rati me jalava diva  hnjuaa de tel da-----


F   F  GA  FFA   AG   AC'   A   G  AGF
hay o rbba  sjna    nu- chhetti kyu nhi melda


sanu ek pl chain na aave....


AA^b   A  AA  A  GAC'A  A^bA
kise da yar n  prdes  jave


 GDF     G  GG  G  AG  DF
vichhoda na kise de pesh aave


sanu ek pl chain na aave....


AA  AAA    A  AC'  AFG  AAA    AG  D  F
rog viyog-2 te  sog hjara  sjna    tere na de


A  G  AG    AA  AC'AGG  GGG   C'AG  GAG  F
ho na bhandi roz kyamt   vichhde ya-r  jina- de


sanu ek pl chain na aave....
```

Vinod Kumar

44. SARA JAGAT PARAYA HAI MA

Mata ki Bhent   Chord: E♭GB♭   S=C #
Taal: Kaharwa
Transpose+1 and play from C Scale
https://wynk.in/music/song/sara-jagat-paraya-hai-maa/sa_INH100701553

jagdamba he jagdamba he sara jagat paraaya he ma

he ma tere dware aaya he ma he ma

janam janam di daasi he ma, he ma tere daras di pyasi

dukh dardaan ne paya ghera, kar de mata dur hanera-2

jaykara tera laya he ma, he ma tere dware aaya

ambe ma tu bhauna vaali, koi na dar ton janda khali-2

tu hi ghat ghat vaasi he ma, he ma tere daras di pyasi

nange pairi akbar aaya, dhyanu bhagat ne sees chadhaya-2

mainnu kyon bisraya he ma, he ma tere dware aaya

mata teri sher sawaari, tun bhagtaan nu bakshan haari-2

muk jaaye lakh chaurasi he ma, he ma tere daras di pyasi

he ma he ma

SARA JAGAT PARAYA HAI MA

dhage nti nkedhin	dhage nti nkedhin	dhage nti nkedhin	dhage nti nkedhin
12 34 56 78	12 34 56 78	12 34 56 78	12 34 56 78

C'C'C'D'   E$^{b'}$ C'C'C'B^b C'
jgdmba   he jgdmba   he

CC   CD.B^b C DE^{b}D C   .A^b
sara jg-t   praya he ma

D   D   DD E^{b}D   CC
he man tere dware aaya

G   GC'B^{b}C'G   F   G
he ma   he ma

CCC   CD.B^b CD E^{b}CD C   .A^b
jnm   jnm di- da-si he ma

D   D DD E^{b}E^{b}D D CC
he ma tere drs   di pyasi

FF   GGA^b B^{b}G FG   C'C'
dukh drda ne- paya ghera

D' D' E$^{b'}$ D'B^b A^{b}B^b D'D'C'
kr de mata-   dur hnera

B^b B^b C'C'   B^b C'C'C'
kr de mata   dur hnera

G   GGF   GG E^{b}D C .A^b
jy kara- tera laya he ma

D   D   DD E^{b}D   CC
he man tere dware aaya

FG   A^b B^{b}G FG   C'C'
ambe man tu- bhauna vali

136

Vinod Kumar

D’D’   D’   D’   D’C’A^b A^{b}B^b D’C’
koii   na dr   to--   janda khali

B^{b}B^b C’ C’ C’   B^{b}B^b C’C’
koii na dr to janda khali

G   G GF GG   E^{b}D   C .A^b
tu hi ght ght vasi he   ma

D   D   DD E^{b}E^{b}D D CC
he man tere drs   di pyasi

FG   A^b B^{b}G   F G   C’C’
nnge pairi- akbr   aaya

D’D’   D’E^b’E^b’ D’B^b A^b B^b D’D’C’
dhyanu bhgt   ne- sis chdhaya

B^{b}B^b C’C’   C’   B^{b}B^b C’C’C’
dhyanu bhgt   ne sis chdhaya

GG   GF   GGE^{b}D   C .A^b
mainnu kyon bisraya he   ma

D   D   DD   E^{b}D   CC
he man tere dware aaya

FG   A^{b}B^{b}G   FG GC’C’
mata teri-   sher svari ,

D’   D’D’D’   D’C’B^b A^b B^b_ D’C’
tu bhgta   nu---   bkshn hari

B^b B^{b}C’   C’   B^{b}B^b C’C’
tu bhgta nu bkshn hari

GG   G GFG   GE^{b}D   C .A^b
muk jae l-kh chorasi he ma

D	D	DD	E♭E♭D	D CC		B♭	C'	B♭	D' C'
he	man	tere	drs	di pyasi		he	ma	he	ma

45. SATGURU MAIN TERI PATANG

Taal: Kaharwa   Chord: DFA   S=C#

Transpose+1 and play from C Scale

https://youtu.be/Sw8WbF4-gMQ

satguru main teri patang, waheguru main teri patang

hawa vich udadi jawangi -2

saaiyaan dor hatthon chhaddi na main katti jawangi

badi mushkil de naal milya mainu tera dwara hai

mainu ikko tera aasra nale tera sahara hai

hun tere hi bharose, hawa vich udadi jawangi

saaiyaan dor hatthon chhaddi na main katti jawangi

aena charna kamlaan nalon mainu dur hatavin na

is jhuthe jag de andar mera pecha laayin na

je kat gayi taan satgur, fir main lutti jawangi

saaiyaan dor hatthon chhaddi na main katti jawangi

aaj maleya buha aahe main tere dwar da

hath rakh de ek vaari tun mere sir te pyaar da

fir janam maran de gede to main bachdi jawangi

saaiyaan dor hatthon chhaddi na main katti jawangi

Vinod Kumar

SATGURU MAIN TERI PATANG

| dha | ge | n | ti | n | ke | dhi | n | dha | ge | n | ti | n | ke | dhi | n |
1	2	3	4	5	6	7	8	1	2	3	4	5	6	7	8
												D	D	D	E
												s	t	gu	ru
C	-	-	D	D	F	E	-	D	-	-	D	D	D	D	E
mai	-	-	te	ri	-	p	-	tn	-	-	g	s	t	gu	ru
C	-	-	D	D	F	E	-	D	-	D	D	D	A	A	A
mai	-	-	te	ri	-	p	-	tn	-	g	h	va	-	vi	ch
A	A	A	-	G	-	F#	-	G	-	-	D	D	A	A	A
u	d	di	-	ja	-	va	-	gi	-	-	h	va	-	vi	ch
A	A	A	-	G	-	F#	-	G	-	-	-	G	-	G	F#
u	d	di	-	ja	-	va	-	gi	-	-	-	sa	ii	yaan	-
G	A	-	G	G	-	F	-	F	-	G	-	E	-	D	C
do	-	-	r	h	t	tho	-	chh	d	di	-	na	-	mai	-
E	-	E	-	F	-	E	-	D	-	-	-				
k	-	tti	-	ja	-	va	-	gi	-	-	-				
														A	A
														b	di
A	A	A	C'	C'	-	B	-	A	-	A	-	-	-	A	A
mu	sh	kl	l	de	-	na	l	mi	l	ya	-	-	-	mai	nu
G	A	-	G	F	-	F	G	G	A	-	-	-	-	F	E
te	ra	-	d	va	-	ra	-	hai	-	-	-	-	-	mai	nu
E	E	-	F	G	F	E	-	D	-	-	-	-	-	A	A
te	ra	-	d	va	-	ra	-	hai	-	-	-	-	-	mai	nu
A	-	A	C'	C'	-	B	-	A	-	-	A	A	-	A	A
i	-	kko	-	te	-	ra	-	aa	-	-	s	ra	-	na	le
G	A	-	G	F	-	F	G	G	A	-	-	-	-	F	E
te	ra	-	s	ha	-	ra	-	hai	-	-	-	-	-	na	le

E	E	-	F	G	F	E	-	D	-	-	-	-	-	D	D
te	ra	-	s	ha	-	ra	-	hai	-	-	-	-	-	hu	n

C	-	D	-	F	-	E	-	D	-	D	-	-	-	D	D
te	-	re	-	hi	-	bh	-	ro	-	se	-	-	-	hu	n

C	-	D	-	F	-	E	-	D	-	D	D	D	A	A	A
te	-	re	-	hi	-	bh	-	ro	-	se	h	va	-	vi	ch

A	A	A	-	G	-	F$^{\#}$	-	G	-	-	-	G	-	G	F$^{\#}$
u	d	di	-	ja	-	va	-	gi	-	-	-	sa	ii	yaan	-

G	A	-	G	G	-	F	-	F	-	G	-	E	-	D	C
do	-	-	r	h	t	tho	-	chh	d	di	-	na	-	mai	-

E	-	E	-	F	-	E	-	D	-	-	-
k	-	tti	-	ja	-	va	-	gi	-	-	-

```
AA    A-AC'  C'-B  AA  AA      GAA  GFFG  GA
aena chr-na- kmla nalo mainu  du-r  htavi-  na-

FE    EE    FGFE   D
mainu dur   htavi-  na

AA  A-AC'     C'B  B  AA  AA    GAG    FFG  GA
is  jhu-the-  jg  de andr mera  pecha  laii-  na-

FE  EEF    GFE   D
mera pecha- laii-   na

D  CC  DDF  E  D-D-        DA  A   AA  GF#G
je kt  gyi-   ta stguru 2,   fer mai lutti  javagi 2,

GGF#  GAG  GF   FG    E  DC  EE  FED
saiiya  do-r  hatho chhddi na, mai-  ktti  javagi

AA  A-AC'     C'-B  AA  A   GA  GF-G   GA
ajj  maleya    bu-ha aake mai  tere dwa-r   da-

FE  EEF    GFE   D
mai- tere- dwa-r  da
```

```
AA  AA AC'  C'B  AA  A  AA      GA  AG  F-G  GA
hth  rkh de-   ek  vari tu mere  sir  te-  pyar  da-

FE    E  EF    GFE  D
mere  sir  te-  pyar  da

D  CC  DDF  FE   D-D-    DA   A   AAA  GF#G
fir jnm  mrn   de-  ge-de- 2 to-  mai bchdi   javagi 2,

GGF#  GAG  GF   FG    E  DC   EE  FED
saiiya  do-r  hatho chhddi na, mai-  ktti  javagi
```

46. SHAWA TAMASHA VANGA DA

Album: Mehndi Shagna di   Chord: DFA   S=C
Taal: Kaharwa   Singer: Sudha Malhotra, Kiran
https://youtu.be/iinCEW5ZNDs

shawa tamasha wangaan da, wah wah tamasha wangaan da
meri gali vich wangaan aaiyaan mainu chadya cha.

sas kolon puchheya nanaan kolon puchheya kise n ditiyan chadha
shawa tamasha wangaan da, wah wah tamasha wangaan da
kise n ditiyaan chadha mere maaiyaan, aape laiyaan chadha

meri gali vich wangaan aaiyaan mainu chadya cha
bahron ta aaya maai hansda hansda, bhabo ne ditta sikha
shawa tamasha wangaan da, wah wah tamasha wangaan da
andar vad one danda chukya, wangaan ditiyaan fanaa

main taa tur hun peke challi aan, bhabo di pakiyaan kha
shawa tamasha wangaan da, wah wah tamasha wangaan da
bhabo di pakiyaan batere wele khaadiyaan teriyaan da hun chaa
shawa tamasha wangaan da, wah wah tamasha wangaan da

bhar bhar ke main wangaan layaanwaan chun chun ke tu pa

shawa tamasha wangaan da, wah wah tamasha wangaan da

chun chun ke main wangaan paawaan tu ankhiyaan nal la

shawa tamasha wangaan da, wah wah tamasha wangaan da

SHAWA TAMASHA VANGA DA

dha	ge	n	ti	n	ke	dhi	n	dha	ge	n	ti	n	ke	dhi	n
1	2	3	4	5	6	7	8	1	2	3	4	5	6	7	8

prelude:
.A D F E D A G F C D F E D- D-
.A D F E D A G F C D F E D- D-
A – AB- C'- D'E' C'D'—C'D' BC' A-G-
G- GA- B- C'-B-GA- GA FG E- D-
D—E F, G—FE, C—D E , D—

E.A .ACD EF F F EC CDE DD D
shava tmasha vnga da, vah vah tmasha vnga da -2

music: D—E F, G—FE, C—D E , D—

DD GG GF GA GF FG FEE D
meri gli vich vnga aaiiyaan mainu chdhya cha

E.A .ACD EF F F EC CDE DD D
shava tmasha vnga da, vah vah tmasha vnga da

music:
F- D- E- C- D- E A G –
B- G- A- F- FG FED—
A-G B-A C'-B AG F-GA GFE D-
F- D- E- C- D- E A G –
B- G- A- F- FG FED—

DD DG GGG FGA AA GGF FG F FEE DD
sas kolo puchhya nnan kolo puchhya, kise n ditiyaan chdha

Vinod Kumar

DD   GGG   GA   G   F   F   G   FEE   DD   D
shava tmasha vnga da   ji, vah vah tmasha vnga da

DD G GGG   FG   AG   FE   FG   FE   DD
kise n ditiyaan chdha mere maiiya, aape liiyaan chdha

E.A .ACD   EF   F   F   EC   CDE   DD   D
shava tmasha vnga da, vah vah tmasha vnga da -2

DD GG GF GA   G F   FG   FEE   D   E.A   .ACD...
meri gli vich vnga aaiiyaan, mainu chdhya   cha, shava tmasha-

DD   G GG G   GAA GFF   FG   F EE   DD
bahro ta aaya maii hnsda hnsda, bhabo ne ditta sikha

DD   GGG   GA   G   F   F   G   FEE   DD   D
shava tmasha vnga da   bhii, vah vah tmasha vnga da

DDG G GF GA GFF   FG   FEE DD E.A   .ACD...
andr vr one dnda chukya, vnga ditiyaan fna, shava   tmasha....

D   D G GF GA   GG F FG   F FEE   D   DD   GG
mai ta tur hun peke chlli aa, bhabo di pkiyaan kha, shava tmash

DD   G GGG   FGA AG GFF   FGG   F   EE   D
bhabo di pkiyaan btere vele khadiyan, teriyaan da hun   cha,

E.A   .ACD...
shava tmasha..

D   D G GF   GA   GGF FG GF   E   E D
bhr bhr ke mai-   vnga lyava, chun chun ke tu pa,

DD   GGG....
shava tmasha...

 D   D G GF   GA   GF F GFE   E   D
chun chun ke mai-   vnga pava, tu ankhiyaan nal la,

E.A   .ACD...
shava tmasha....

47. SUHE VACHIRE VALEYA

Taal: Kaharwa Dugun
Transpose+1 and play from C Scale
https://youtu.be/ksFE7DmAhsl

Singer: Surinder Kaur
Chord: DFA   S=C#

suhe vacheere vaaleya main kahni aan
kar chhatri di chhaan main chhaanve baini aan

suhe vacheere vaaleya ful kikraan de
kikraan laayi bahaar mele mitraan de

suhe vacheere vaaleya ful tori da
baaj tere ve maahiya kuj nahin lodi da

suhe vacheere vaaleya main kahni aan
lagde teer judaaiyaan de main sahni aan

suhe vacheere vaaleya do laladiyaan,
mela vekhan aaiyaan karmaa waaladiyaan

suhe vacheere vaaleya dhan jodi da,
dil da najuk shisha inj nahin todi da

sau sau pain dalilaan charkha daai da
ik vaari aake tak ja, haal judaayi da

suhe vacheere vaaleya gal gaani aan
charkha rang rangeela vehde jaani aan

suhe vacheere vaaleya main kahni aan
kar chhatri di chhaan main chhaanve bahni aan

Vinod Kumar

SUHE VACHIRE VALEYA

dhage	nti	nkedhin	dhage	nti	nkedhin	dhage	nti	nkedhin	dhage	nti	nkedhin
12	34	56 78	12	34	56 78	12	34	56 78	12	34	56 78

prelude: E A G F E G
^{F} E G F E D F
E D E E F E
^{D} E F E E E

EE   GGG   A AG   G   FF   E
suhe vchire valeya, mai khni aa

EF   FFF   F   E   D   E G   FF   E
kr   chhtri   di chha, mai chhave bhni aa

music: F F F F E -- ^{D} E G F F E

EE   GGG   A AG   G   F F   E
suhe vchire valeya, ful   kikra   de

F F   F   EE D EG   F F   E
kikra layi, bhar   mele mitra   de

EE   GGG   A AG   G   FF   E
suhe vchire valeya, full   tori   da

F FF   F E E   E   G   FF   E
baj tere ve mahiya, kuj ni   lodi   da

EE   GGG   A AG   G   F F   E
suhe vchire valeya, mai   khni   aa

F F   F   EEE   E   G   FF   E
lgde   tir judaiyaan de mai shni aa

EE   GGG   A AG   G   F F E
suhe vchire valeya, do laldiyaan

F F   FF   EE   E G   F F E
mela vekhn aaiiaa krma valadiyaan

```
EE   GGG  A AG   G  FF  E
suhe vchire valeya, dhn jodi da


F     F  FF  E E      E   G  FF   E
dil   da najuk shiisha, inj  nhi todi  da


E   E  GG  G GA  G G  FF  E
sau sau pain dlila  chrkha daii da


F F     FF  E  E    EG  GFF  E
ik vari aake tk  ja,  hal  judaii  da


EE   GGG  A AG   G  FF   E
suhe vchire valeya,  gl  gani  aa


F F     F   FEE   E G   FF   E
chrkha rng rngila, vehde jani aa


EE  GGG   A AG   G  F F   E
suhe vchire valeya,  mai  khni  aa,


EF  FFF   F  E    D    E G    FF  E
kr   chhtri  di chha, mai chhave bhni aa
```

Vinod Kumar

48. SUHE VACHIRE VALEYA

Taal: Kaharwa Dugun
Transpose+1 and play from C Scale
https://youtu.be/9XwLGvaiL9g

Singer: Musarrat Nazir
Chord: CEG   S=C#

suhe vacheere vaaleya main kahni aan
kar chhatri di chhaan main chhaanve bahni aan

ma peyaan ne chun leya saathi tainnu mera
jindadi to pyara hun pyar mainnu tera
rakh kadmaan de naal main pairi paini aan

pahli vaari tere kolon ik wada laina
hun tu hamesha mere dil vich raina
jag bhul ke din raat main na tera laini aan
kar chhatri di chhaan main chhaanve bahni aan

main chhankaaiyaan tere vede vich chudiyaan
mangiyaan muradaan aj ho gaiyaan puriyaa
kadi na todi saath main tainnu kahni aan
kar chhatri di chhaan main chhaanve bahni aan

SUHE VACHIRE VALEYA

dhage	nti	nkedhin	dhage	nti	nkedhin	dhage	nti	nkedhin	dhage	nti	nkedhin
12	34	56 78	12	34	56 78	12	34	56 78	12	34	56 78

prelude:
EF EG FF EE, EF EG FF E-

EE   GGG A AG G FF E
suhe vchire valeya, mai khni aa

EF   FFF F E   D   E G FF E
kr   chhtri di chha, mai chhave bhni aa

music: EF EG FF EE, EF EG FF E-

E GA   B AA EF AG   FE EE
man peyaan ne chun leya sathi tennu mera

EGA B AA EF AG   FE EE
jinddi to pyara hun pyar mainnu tera

EG GGG G GAA A GG FF E
rkh kdman de na-l mai pairi paini aa

EF   FFF   F E   D   E G   FF E
kr   chhtri di chha, mai chhave bhni aa

music: EF EG FF EE, EF EG FF E-

EG AB AA EF   AG FE EE
phli vari tere kolo ik vada laina

EG A BAA EF   AG FE EE
hun tu hmesha mere dil vich raina

EG GG G GF# GAA A G GG FF E
jg bhul ke din ra-t mai na tera laini aa

EF   FFF   F E   D   E G   FF E
kr   chhtri di chha, mai chhave bhni aa

Vinod Kumar

music: EF EG FF EE, EF EG FF E-

EG   AB AA   EF AG   FE   EEE
mai   chhrkayiyaan tere vede vich chudiyaan

EGA   BAA   EF AG FE   EEE
mngiyaan muradaa aj   ho- giyaan puriyaan

EG   G GGF$^\#$ GAA A   GG   FF   E
kdi   na todi-   sa-th mai tainnu khni   aa

EF   FFF   F E   D   E G   FF E
kr   chhtri di chha, mai chhave bhni aa

49. TERE BIN NAI LAGDA

Taal: Kaharwa

Transpose+1 and play from C Scale

https://youtu.be/f6uRxh2l0l4

Singer: Nusarat Fateh Ali

Chord: .G.B^{b}D   S=C#

jaan e khuda, meharbaa tere siwa kaun mera
kadi na hovin juda, todi na saath mera
jaaniyaan haaniyaan -2

tu vi sikh kadi dukh sukh folna
tere bin tere bin
tere bin nahi lagda dil mera dholna -2
puchh kaare badraan to seene vich aag lag
langh gaiyaan kai barsaataan-2
tur gayo sajna niindraan kho ke
jaag ke katiyaan raataan
aa vi ja na sataa vastaa pyar da
ae ruttaan sohneya mud nahi aaniyaan
tere bin tere bin
tere bin nahi lagda dil mera dholna -2

dil tainnu de baithi khabre tu aisse layi
karna e be parwaaiyaan
kiite vaade qasamaan tainu yaad kade nahi aaiyaan
ae gila pyar da khol aas zara
tarse naina te kar meharbaaniyaan
tere bin tere bin
tere bin nahi lagda dil mera dholna -2

Vinod Kumar

TERE BIN NAI LAGDA

dha	ge	n	ti	n	ke	dhi	n	dha	ge	n	ti	n	ke	dhi	n
1	2	3	4	5	6	7	8	1	2	3	4	5	6	7	8

```
 G  G  GF#    F# E     GG  GF#   F#F  DDb ....... C.BbC .Bb
jan e khuda, mehrban tere siva,  kaun  mera---------------

.G.G  .Bb   D D    DDb   C.Bb  .F#-- .G  DDbD C  .G.Bb
kdi    na  honvi juda,  todi  na ----     sa---th  mera

DFFG --- F#GFD   DFFG  --- F#GFD
janiyaan             haniya,

DFFG      DFFG
janiyaan  haniya

D  D  GG   GG   FG   FE  F- EDC
tu vi  sikh  kdi  dukh  sukh  fo-lna-

.G  .Bb    .G   .Bb
tere bin..  tere  bin

.G  .Bb   C   DC   .Bb  CD--    CCC
tere bin nii  lgda   dil  mera   dholna

.G  .Bb   C   DC   .Bb  CD   .Bb.Bb.Bb
tere bin nii  lgda   dil  mera   dholna

 DD        DbD  .G.BbD  D   DD  DbD  .G.Bb    DD
puchchha kare  bdra     to  sine vich   ag      lg

.F#.F#   .F#.F#     Db   C.Bb.G.Bb-- CD
lngh     giiyaan  kaii  brsata         -2

.Bb CD  EEE   DCED      D   D
tur gyo sjna    nindraan   kho ke

.BbC  D  EEDC  DF
jag   ke ktiyaan  rata
```

D   D   A^b G   FG   DDA^b GF   G – D
aa   vi   ja   na   sta   vasta   pyar   da

F   FG- E   EEF-D   D   D   CEED
e   ruta   sohneya   mur naii aaniyaan

.G   .B^b .G   .B^b
tere bin..   tere   bin

.G   .B^b C   DC   .B^b CD--   CCC
tere bin nii lgda   dil mera   dholna

.G   .B^b C   DC   .B^b CD   .B^b.B^b.B^b
tere bin nii lgda   dil mera   dholna

D   D^{b}D   .G.B^b D^{b}D   DDD^b D   .G.B^b D^{b}D
dil tainnu   de   baithi khbre tu   esse   laii

.F$^\#$.F$^\#$ .F$^\#$ D^b C.B^b.G.B^b – CD-.B^b
krna   e   be-prvaiiyaan-----------

.B^{b}C   EE   DCE   DD   .B^{b}C   DE   DC   D F
kiite vade ksman tainnu yad   kde   naii aaiiyaan

D   DA^b GF   G   DD   A^{b}G   FG
ae gila pyar da khol   aas   zra

FF   GE   E   F   DDC-EED
trse naina te kr mehrbaniyaan

.G   .B^b .G   .B^b
tere bin..   tere   bin

.G   .B^b C   DC   .B^b CD-- CCC
tere bin nii lgda   dil mera dholna

.G   .B^b C   DC   .B^b CD   .B^b.B^b.B^b
tere bin nii lgda   dil mera   dholna

Vinod Kumar

50. TERI MURALI DI MITHI

Taal: Kaharwa   Chord: FA^{b}C' E^{b}GB^b S=C#

Transpose+1 and play from C Scale

teri murali di -2 mitthi mitthi taan te, taan te

main taa ho ho gayi qurbaan ve

main taa ho gayi ho gayi ho gayi qurbaan ve

murali vajaa ke haay dil sada lai gayaa

ankh de ishare naal sab kuj kah gaya

hun jiniyaa main lai lai teraa naam ve naam ve

main taa ho ho gayi qurbaan ve

chhaddi na umar bhar kadi mera saath ve

aave na vichhode vali kadi shyama raat ve

tere kadmaa ch meri jind jaan ve

main taa ho ho gayi qurbaan ve

kar gaye ghaayal naina vaale teer ve

pyar tera pake meri khuli taqdir ve

hove kadmaa ch zindagi di shaam ve

main taa ho ho gayi qurbaan ve

TERI MURALI DI MITHI

dhage	nti	nke	dhin	dhage	nti	nke	dhin	dhage	nti	nke	dhin	dhage	nti	nke	dhin
12	34	56	78	12	34	56	78	12	34	56	78	12	34	56	78
prelude: A^{b}A^b GF A^{b}A^b GF A^{b}A^b GF G---															
A^{b}A^b GF A^{b}A^b GF A^{b}A^b GF F---															
						F		F	-C'	-	C'	-	-	F	F
						te		ri	mur	-li	-	di	-	- te	ri
F	-C'	-	C'	C'	C'	B^b	A	B^b	-	-	A^b	G	F	-	-
mur	-li	-	di	mi	thi	mi	thi	ta	-	-	n	te	-	-	-
B^b	-	-	A^b	G	F	E^b	E^b	F	-	G	-	A^b	- G	F	
ta	-	-	n	te	-	mai	ta	ho	-	ho	-	g	ii ku	r	

G	F	-	F	F	G	E♭	E♭	F	F	G	G	A♭	A♭	G	F
ba	-	-	n	ve	-	mai	ta	ho	gii	ho	gii	ho	gii	ku	r

G	F	-	F	F	-
ba	-	-	n	ve	-

interlude: A♭A♭ GF A♭A♭ GF A♭A♭ GF G---
         A♭A♭ GF A♭A♭ GF A♭A♭ GF F- A♭- C'-

C'F'	F'	F'	E♭'	E♭'	D'	B♭	D'	D'	F'	F'	D♭'	C'	C'	-
mur	li	v	ja	ke	ha	y	di	l	sa	da	lai	-g	ya	-

-	A♭A♭	A♭	A♭	B♭	B♭	G	F	-	E♭F	-G	-G	F	F	F	-
-	ankh	de	i	sha	re	na	l	-	sb	-ku	-j	kh	-g	ya	-

-	-	F	F	-	FC'	C'	C'	C'	C'	B♭	A	B♭	-	-	A♭
-	-	hu	n	-	jini	yaan	mai	lai	lai	te	ra	na	-	-	m

G	F	-	-	B♭	-	-	A♭	G	F	E♭	E♭	F	-	G	-
ve	-	-	-	na	-	-	m	ve	-	mai	ta	ho	-	ho	-

A♭	-	G	F	G	F	-	F	F	G	E♭	E♭	F	F	G	G
g	ii	ku	r	ba	-	-	n	ve	-	mai	ta	ho	gii	ho	gii

A♭	A♭	G	F	G	F	-	F	F	-
ho	gii	ku	r	ba	-	-	n	ve	-

C'	F'F'	F'	E♭'	E♭'	D'	B♭	-	D'D'	F'	F'	D♭'	C'	C'	-
chh	ddi,na	u	m	r	bh	r	-	kdi	-me	-ra	sa	th	ve	-

-	A♭	A♭A♭	A♭	B♭	B♭	G	F	-	E♭F	-G	-G	F	F	F	-
-	aa	ve,na	-vi	chho	de	va	li	-	kdi	-shyama	ra	-t	ve	-

-	-	F	F	-	FC'	C'	C'	C'	C'	B♭	A	B♭	-	-	A♭
-	-	te	re	-	kd	man	ch	me	ri	jin	d	ja	-	-	n

G	F	-	-	B♭	-	-	A♭	G	F	E♭	E♭	F	-	G	-
ve	-	-	-	ja	-	-	n	ve	-	mai	ta	ho	-	ho	-

A♭	-	G	F	G	F	-	F	F	G	E♭	E♭	F	F	G	G
g	ii	ku	r	ba	-	-	n	ve	-	mai	ta	ho	gii	ho	gii

Vinod Kumar

A♭	A♭	G	F	G	F	-	F	F	-
ho	gii	ku	r	ba	-	-	n	ve	-

	C'F'	F'	F'	E♭'	-	D'	B♭	-	D'	D'F'	F'	D♭'	C'	C'	-
	kr	g	ye	gha	-	y	l	-	nai	na,va	-le	ti	-r	ve	-

-	A♭	A♭A♭	A♭	B♭	B♭	G	F	-	E♭F	-G	-G	F	F	F	-
-	pya	r,te	ra	pa	ke	me	ri	-	khulli	-t	k	di	r	ve	-

-	-	F	F	-	FC'	C'	C'	C'	C'	B♭	A	B♭	-	-	A♭
-	-	ho	ve	-	kd	man	ch	zin	d	gi	di	sha	-	-	m

G	F	-	-	B♭	-	-	A♭	G	F	E♭	E♭	F	-	G	-
ve	-	-	-	sha	-	-	m	ve	-	mai	ta	ho	-	ho	-

A♭	-	G	F	G	F	-	F	F	G	E♭	E♭	F	F	G	G
g	ii	ku	r	ba	-	-	n	ve	-	mai	ta	ho	gii	ho	gii

A♭	A♭	G	F	G	F	-	F	F	-
ho	gii	ku	r	ba	-	-	n	ve	-

51. UDA AADA EEDI SASSA

Old Punjabi Song   Singer: Narinder Biba, Maan
Lyrics: Gurudev Singh Maan   Chord: CEG   S=D
Taal: Kaharwa
Transpose+2 and play from C Scale
https://www.youtube.com/watch?v=EEcN6RwKkBY
(Old Song)

uda aada eedi sassa haha uda aada ho

mainnu jaan de sakule ik vaar hada ve

    o tainka thatha dadda dhadda dadda dhadda nana ni

    ni tu mud chal ghar nai sakule jana ni

ve main tere naal diljani rus jaavangi

na main ridkaangi dudh te na roti lavaangi

kakka khakkha gagga ghaggha oye mere beliya

kakka khakkha gagga ghaggha gagga ghaggha nanna ve

mainnu lai de ik kaida na chadhavin vangaan ve

    ni tu ja ke sakule das ki karengi

    meri lado mainnu dass othe ki tu padhengi

    tatta thattha dadda dhaddha- o meriye hanade

    tatta thattha dadda dhaddha dadda dhaddha nanna ni

    ni tu mudadi ae ki nahin tere gitte bhanna ni

aa ja vekh mere maahi ve main ki karaangi

ve main dharti sanwar ke te inj padhangi

chacha chhachha jajja jhajja o mere haaniya

chacha chhachha jajja jhajja jajja jhajja nanna ve

ve tu khetaan val chal main sakule vanjaan ve

    je tu meri bholi bhaliye ni padh jaanvengi

    ni tun chitthiyaan begaaneyaan nu likh paanvengi

    pappa faffa babba bhaba………

    o pappa faffa babba bhaba babba bhaba mamma ni

    tera ronda rahe jo mahi lamm te salamma ni-2

Vinod Kumar

tu vi padh mere likkhe tainnu khat aun ge

bhed jaan ke talange tainnu nas jaan ge

yayya rara lalla vava—mere beliya

yayya rara lalla vava lalla vava dhadha ve

"maan" dove challiye sakule ae nahin kamm mada ve-2

UDA AADA EEDI SASSA

dhage	nti	nkedhin	dhage	nti	nkedhin	dhage	nti	nkedhin	dhage	nti	nkedhin
12	34 56 78		12	34 56 78		12	34 56 78		12	34 56 78	

```
EE    FG    FF   EE   EE   EE    DE   F
uda  aada  iidi sssa haha uda  aada  ve


EE      FG  F EEE  DE   FG FE   E
mainnu jan de skule  ik   var hada ve


      E EE  FG    FF   EE EE   EE   DE  F
      o tainka ththa dda  dhda dda dhda nana ni


      E  E  FG FE   EE   D   EFG  FF  E
      ni  tu mur chl ghr  nii  skule janna ni


E   E  FG  FE  EE DE    FG    FEE
ve  mai tere nal dil jani   rus    javagi


E   E  FGFE     EE  D  E  FG    FEE
na  mai rirkangi dudh te na  roti    lavagi


F#G    F#G    F#G   F#G   A   GG   F#GF#G – FE
kkka  khkkha  ggga  ghgga  oye mere beliya


EE    FG    FF    EE    EE   EE   DE   F
kkka  khkkha ggga  ghgga  ggga ghgga nnna ve


EE     F  G FF  EE   E   EFG     FF  E
mainu lai de ik  kaida na  chdhavin vnga ve
```

E E   FG F   EEE DE   FG FEE
ni tu ja ke skule ds   kii   krengi

EE   FG   FE   EE   DE   F G   FEE
meri lado mainnu dass othe kii tu pdhengi

F#G F#G   F#G F#G   A   GG   F#G F#G – FE
ttta   thttha ddda dhdda- o meriye hanne

E EE FG   FF   EE   EE   EE   DE   F
o   ttta thttha ddda dhdda ddda dhdda nnna ni

E E   FG   F F EE   DE FG   FE   E
ni tu murdi ae kii nhi tere gitte bhnna ni

E E FG   FF EE   D E FG FEE
aa ja vekh mere mahi ve mai kii krangi

E E   FGF EEE D E FG FEE
ve mai dhrti snvar ke te inj pdhangi

F#G   F#G   F#G F#G A GG   F#G F#G – FE
chchcha chhchchha jjja   jhjja   o mereya haniya

EE   FG   FF EE EE EE DE   F
chchcha chhchchha jjja   jhjja jjja jhjja nnna ve

E E FG   FE EE E EFG   FE   E
ve tu kheta vl   chl mai sakule vnjan ve

E E FG FF   EED   E FG FEE
je tu meri bholi bhaliye   ni pdh javengi

E E FGF   EEE F   G FG   FEE
ni tu chitthiyaan beganeyaan nu likh pavengi

F#G F#G F#G   F#G
pppa fffa   bbba bhbba------

Vinod Kumar

E EE FG FF   EE   EE EE   DE   F
o, pppa fffa bbba bhbba bbba bhbba mmma ni

EE FG   F   E EE DE   F GFE   E
tera ronda rhe jo mahi lamm te salmma ni -2

E E FG   FE   EE   EFG   FG   FE E
tu vi pdh mere likkhe tainnu   khat aun ge

DE FG   F EEE   EFG   FG FE E
bhed jan ke talange tainnu   ns jan ge

F#G   F#G   F#G   F#G   A GG F#G F#G FE
yyya rara   llla   vava—o mere beliya

EE FG FF EE EE EE   DE   F
yyya rara llla vava llla vava dada ve

 EE   FGF   EEE E E FG   FE E
"man" (dove) chlliye skule ae nhi kmm mada ve -2

52.   SARGAM OR ALANKAR OR PALTE

C D E F G A B C'

C' B A G F E D C

CC DD EE FF GG AA BB C'C'

C'C' BB AA GG FF EE DD CC

CCC DDD EEE FFF GGG AAA BBB C'C'C'

C'C'C' BBB AAA GGG FFF EEE DDD CCC

CD DE EF FG GA AB BC'

C'B BA AG GF FE ED DC

CDE- DEF- EFG- FGA GAB- ABC'-

C'BA- BAG- AGF- GFE- FED- EDC-

CDEF DEFG EFGA FGAB GABC'

C'BAG BAGF AGFE GFED FEDC

CDEFG DEFGA EFGAB FGABC'

C'BAGF BAGFE AGFED GFEDC

CE DF EG FA GB AC'

C'A BG AF GE FD EC

Vinod Kumar

CF DG EA FB GC'

C'G BF AE GD FC

CG DA EB FC'

C'F BE AD GC

CA DB EC'

C'E BD AC

CDCDE– DEDEF– EFEFG- FGFGA– GAGAB– ABABC'-

C'BC'BA- BABAG– AGAGF– GFGFE–FEFED– EDEDC-

CDECDCDE DEFDEDEF EFGEFEFG

FGAFGFG GABGAGA ABC'ABABC'

C'BAC'BC'BA BAGBABAG AGFAGAGF

GFEGFGFE FEFEFED EDCEDEDC

C

C D C

C D E D C

C D E F E D C

C D E F G F E D C

C D E F G A G F E D C

C D E F G A B A G F E D C

C D E F G A B C' C' B A G F E D C

C'

C' B C'

C' B A B C'

C' B A G A B C'

C' B A G F G A B C'

C' B A G F E F G A B C'

C' B A G F E D E F G A B C'

C' B A G F E D C D E F G A B C'

C-CDE- D-DEF- E-EFG- F-FGA- G-GAB- A-ABC'-

C'-C'BA- B-BAG- A-AGF- G-GFE- F-FED- E-EDC-

DC ED FE GF AG BA C'B D'C'

BC' AB GA FG EF DE CD .BC

CED DFE EGF FAG GBA AC'B BD'C'

C'AB BGA AFG GEF FDE ECD D.BC

.G.G .A.A .B.B C'C' D'D' E'E' F'F'

F'F' E'E' D'D' C'C' .B.B .A.A .G.G

C D^b E^b F G A^b B^b C'

C' B^b A^b G F E^b D^b C

C D^b E F G A^b B C'

C' B A^b G F E D^b C

53. OTHER BOOKS OF VINOD KUMAR

"mukesh songs' western notes, part -1,2 "

"lata songs' western notes"

"asha songs' western notes"

"suman kalyanpur songs' western notes"

"kishore songs' western notes, part -1,2"

"md. rafi songs' western notes, part -1,2,3,4 "

"singer sachindev burman and yesudas songs' western notes"

"manna dey songs' western notes"

"composer sachindev burman songs' western notes, part -1 "

"kumar shanu songs' western notes"

"superhit 51 gazals' western notes"

"bhajan western notes, part-1,2,3"

'sabad aur punjabi songs' western notes'

These Books are also available in English SRGM and Western CDEFG style at notionpress.com and amazon.in and at Flipkart.com

For English SRGM books search… (Singer name) 51 Songs' Sargam, book.

For Western CDEFG books search… (Singer name) Songs' Western Notes, book.

vinod kumar (vinod66vk@gmail.com)

Vinod Kumar

Scan below QR Code from your mobile to get Vinod Kumar's (Singer name) 51 Songs' Sargam books from Flipkart.com site . (Hindi, English, Western all)

Scan below QR Code from your mobile to get Vinod Kumar's (Singer name) 51 Songs' Sargam books from Amazon.in site . (Hindi, English, Western all)

Hindi S R G M

English SRGM

And

Western CDEF

All type books

www.ingramcontent.com/pod-product-compliance
Lightning Source LLC
Chambersburg PA
CBHW041202150726
48006CB00016B/2083